The Texanist

Charles N. Prothro Texana Series

THE TEXANIST

Fine Advice on Living in Texas

David Courtney and **Jack Unruh**

University of Texas Press
AUSTIN

Copyright © 2017 *Texas Monthly*
All illustrations copyright © Jack Unruh
All rights reserved
Printed in the United States of America
First edition, 2017

The Texanist® is a registered trademark of *Texas Monthly*.

The essays in *The Texanist* were originally published in
slightly altered form in *Texas Monthly*.

Requests for permission to reproduce material
from this work should be sent to:
    Permissions
    University of Texas Press
    P.O. Box 7819
    Austin, TX 78713-7819
    http://utpress.utexas.edu/index.php/rp-form

The paper used in this book meets the minimum
requirements of ANSI/NISO Z39.48-1992 (R1997)
(Permanence of Paper). ∞

Design by Lindsay Starr

Library of Congress Cataloging-in-Publication Data

Names: Courtney, David (Editor), author. | Unruh, Jack, illustrator.
Title: The Texanist : fine advice on living in Texas / David Courtney, Jack Unruh.
Other titles: Texas monthly (Austin, Tex).
Description: First edition. | Austin : University of Texas Press, 2017.
Identifiers: LCCN 2016041693 | ISBN 978-1-4773-1297-1 (cloth : alk. paper)
Subjects: LCSH: Texas—Social life and customs. | Newspapers—Sections, columns,
    etc.—Humor.
Classification: LCC F391.2 .C68 2017 | DDC 976.4—dc23
LC record available at https://lccn.loc.gov/2016041693

For my wife, Kendall, and daughter, Sarah

Contents

Acknowledgments

The Texanist would not have been possible without Evan Smith, who took a chance and hired me at *Texas Monthly*; Jake Silverstein, who edited the columns for the entirety of his tenure at *Texas Monthly* and always pushed me to be a better Texanist; and *Texas Monthly* creative director T. J. Tucker, who had the vision to have the columns illustrated by Jack Unruh in the first place.

I must also thank editor-in-chief Brian D. Sweany, who inherited the Texanist when he took the helm at *Texas Monthly* and has guided the column with a steady hand ever since; former and current *Texas Monthly* fact-checkers, David Moorman, Valerie Wright, Paul Knight, and Christian Wallace, who prevented me from unintentionally making a fool of myself; and former and current *Texas Monthly* copyeditors, Kristen Remeza, Jessie Hunnicutt, Megan Giller, Courtney Bond, Shannon Stahl, and Stacy Hollister, all of whom, on occasion, let me get away with grammatical murder.

Thanks also to *Texas Monthly* art department wizards past and present, Caleb Bennett, Brian Johnson, Andi Beierman, Nicki Longoria, Emily Kimbro, Victoria Millner, and Claire Hogan.

Cathy Casey handled the complicated rights and permissions that made this book possible, and I thank her for her guidance.

And without Casey Kittrell, at the University of Texas Press, this book would not exist. Thank you, Casey.

Most importantly, I have to thank my co-author Jack Unruh, without whom the Texanist wouldn't have been the same. I also owe an enormous debt of gratitude to Jack's wife, Judy Whalen, who made this project a reality. ★

Introduction

The Texanist was born in 2007 as a result of the discontinuation of a *Texas Monthly* column known as "Encyclopedia Texanica," which had been deftly authored by longtime senior editor Anne Dingus. It was to be a humor column disguised as a traditional-style advice column, but with the purpose of providing actual Texcentric assistance and information in the course of what would hopefully be an amusing read.

I never expected to be the Texanist. I had originally been hired as a fact-checker, but looking back, my bona fides—Texas-born to Texas-born parents, Texas-raised, Texas-schooled, and Texas-traveled, with a fluency in the language of Texas, the culture of Texas, and the overall Texanness of both Texas and Texans—were enough that the new job and I turned out to be perfectly suited for one another.

Since the column's debut, it has been my estimable pleasure to serve the citizens of the Lone Star State as a giver of good guidance and the arbiter of what passes for proper conduct in this part of the world—and what does not. And over that time, I'm happy to have advised the hundreds of folks who've found their way to me with all manner of conundrums; the range of topics I've covered in this endeavor, as you will see, is really quite mindboggling. But then Texans are a unique people, and as such bring with them some very unique predicaments.

At the outset, *Texas Monthly* creative director T. J. Tucker, in a stroke of genius, assigned the artwork for the page to legendary Dallas illustrator Jack Unruh. It was a match made in heaven, and, over the course of nine years, Jack provided 105 excellent works of art. I truly believe that the column would not have enjoyed the popularity or longevity that it has without Jack, whose one-of-kind visual contributions brought all those various predicaments to life so whimsically on the page.

Jack was a big damn deal in the commercial art world. Over his long career, his artwork appeared in *National Geographic, Time, Rolling Stone, Sports Illustrated, GQ, Field & Stream,* and *Texas Monthly,* among many other publications. And one year before our paths even crossed, back in 2007, he'd already been inducted into the Society of Illustrators Hall of Fame, with the likes of Norman Rockwell, Al Hirschfeld, Maurice Sendak, and N. C. Wyeth.

His subjects were wide-ranging: Winston Churchill, FDR, JFK, F. Scott Fitzgerald, Mark Twain, Muddy Waters, Bob Dylan, Lyle Lovett, Steve Jobs, Julia Louis-Dreyfus, and Khalid Sheikh Mohammed, as well as Native Americans, cowboys, sportsmen, horses, cattle, fish, frogs, birds, deer, rabbits—just about everything under the sun and moon. He once illustrated a translation of Pablo Neruda's *Art of Birds.*

Our working relationship went something like this: At the beginning of each issue, I'd send him the question that was to be illustrated. He'd ruminate on it for a while, send some sketches, and then request reference photos of my face: seething at the sight of broken bottles of Dublin Dr Pepper; violently sneezing, overcome with cedar fever; gleefully polishing off a barbecued rib. In a few weeks, the art department would receive the original illustration, every one full of the fine detail and imaginative brilliance that was his hallmark.

Remarkably, Jack and I only met in person one time, at a book signing for Bill Wittliff in 2014. Jack had contributed illustrations for *The Devil's Backbone*, Wittliff's debut novel, and he was in Austin for the event. Up until that point, he'd seen me only in those reference photos. At our introduction we hugged like long-lost friends, and as we stepped back from our embrace, I noticed Jack intently studying me from various angles. I think he was making mental notes on my overall mien, my skeletal structure, and every crevice and pockmark on my face. Had he gotten me right? He had, every time. Even when he drew me in a tiny bikini bottom or wearing a homecoming gown and tiara.

Shortly after Jack died, in May 2016, following a mercifully short battle with esophageal cancer, his wife, Judy Whalen, graciously invited me to visit his studio, which was located in a building behind their Dallas home. It was a beautiful space, a comfortable upstairs spot full of natural light, inspirational ephemera and curios, sketches, and lots of reference imagery. There, next to a window was his drawing table, just as he had left it. And there was the Texanist, in a pencil sketch that had the face precisely cut out and replaced with a slightly different expression. To the end, he was meticulous with his craft. The result of that effort, the illustration that accompanied the June 2016 Texanist column, was the last piece that he ever completed.

Being the Texanist has been a fun and unique honor, and it has been a great privilege to have been part of the superb and inimitable body of work Jack Unruh left us with.

The following pages contain a handpicked selection of illustrations and the corresponding questions and replies that inspired them. I hope they will make you smile. ⋆

The Texanist

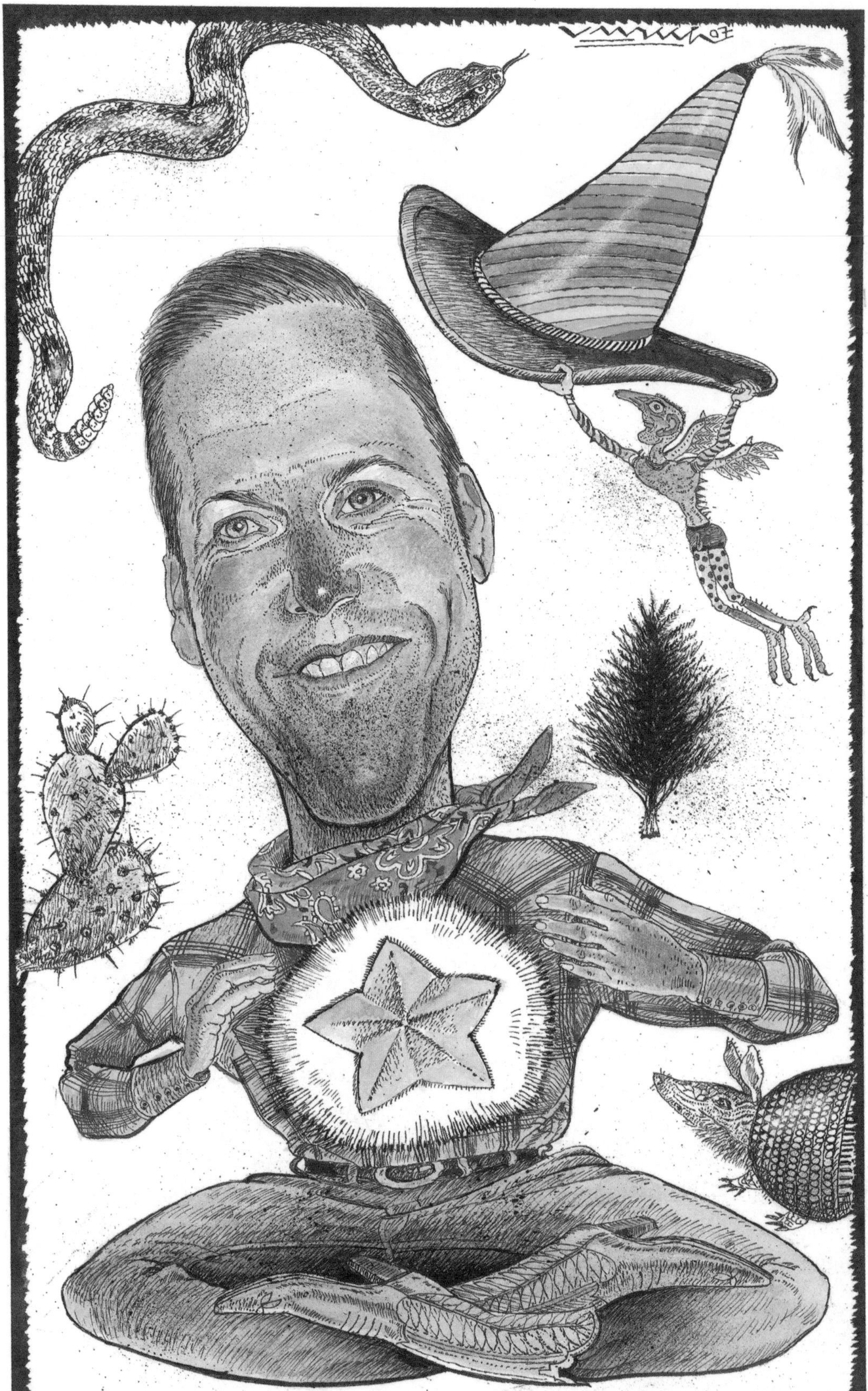

Q: I was born and raised in Texas until age eight and then moved to Pittsburgh, after which I went to college in Arizona. Now living and working in New York City, I am confused as to the proper answer when asked, "Where are you from?" KATE VON DER PORTEN, NEW YORK CITY

A: It is your birthright to claim Texas as your place of origin, and you are absolutely right to do so proudly when asked. Unlike Stephen F. Austin, Sam Houston, George W. Bush, and a mess of other so-called Texans, you were actually born here. Furthermore, you resided here until the ripe old age of 8, by which point, if your childhood was anything like the Texanist's, you had engaged in such authentic local rituals as plinking cans off cedar fence posts, taking sips of your dad's Lone Star, and riding your Schwinn in the cloud behind the DDT truck.

The answer to the question, "Where are you from?" can vary greatly depending on where you are when asked. Like "Mean" Joe Greene, the Texanist was born and raised in Temple. When in Austin, home for more than half his life, he tends to say, "Temple." But on a plane to Los Angeles, he might say, "Austin." If he were to find himself abroad, he would likely say, "Texas." Some people, like the Texanist's father, feel no such need to make adjustments. When posed this question, he would often respond, "Temple born, Temple bred, and when I die I'll be Temple dead."

New York City is full of people, like yourself, who hail from elsewhere. Utah. Arizona. Iowa. Imagine the looks of boredom those people receive when they state their birthplaces. The Texanist would venture a guess that few are the Manhattan dinner parties to have been brightened by the description of an Oklahoma upbringing. You, on the other hand, are fortunate, Ms. von der Porten. You are from Texas. ★

Q: I work for a technology company in a nice office in Austin—despite what you have heard, we are required to wear shoes. Anyway, I have a co-worker who dips Copenhagen and spits into a Styrofoam cup. Is this acceptable in an office environment? MIKE, VIA E-MAIL

A: Though the Texanist cannot condone the use of any product that, according to its own label, "may cause gum disease and tooth loss," he understands well the satisfaction gained from a pinch of moist smokeless tobacco. In youth, he once repaired to the vacant lot behind the Bonanza Steakhouse in Temple with a trusted friend, cut open a fistful of tea bags, and placed this reasonable-seeming tobacco facsimile in a couple of old empty snuff cans. The next day's invitation-only dip at Cater Elementary School resulted in a somewhat jangly buzz—caffeine- rather than nicotine-fueled as it was—and, ultimately, a trip to the principal's office, but the hook had set. Who could have known that a lipful of Lipton would be the gateway to grapevine smoking, Red Man Plug, boxes of San Antonio–made Travis Club Senators, cigarettes by the carton, and an unquenchable thirst for double macchiatos?

But the Texanist digresses. Unlike the husky-voiced and ashy-complexioned throngs who are now fixtures outside every office building, your co-worker has yet to be legally banished for his vice, and until secondhand spittle is shown to cause warts and liver rot, it is unlikely he will be. But while his habit may not inflict actual bodily harm upon bystanders, some are surely discomfited by his amber currents of drool and foul-smelling forgotten spittoons. Your colleague should be mindful of this and employ discretion, confining his dips to the men's room or his own desk. The office is not the horseshoe court. ✦

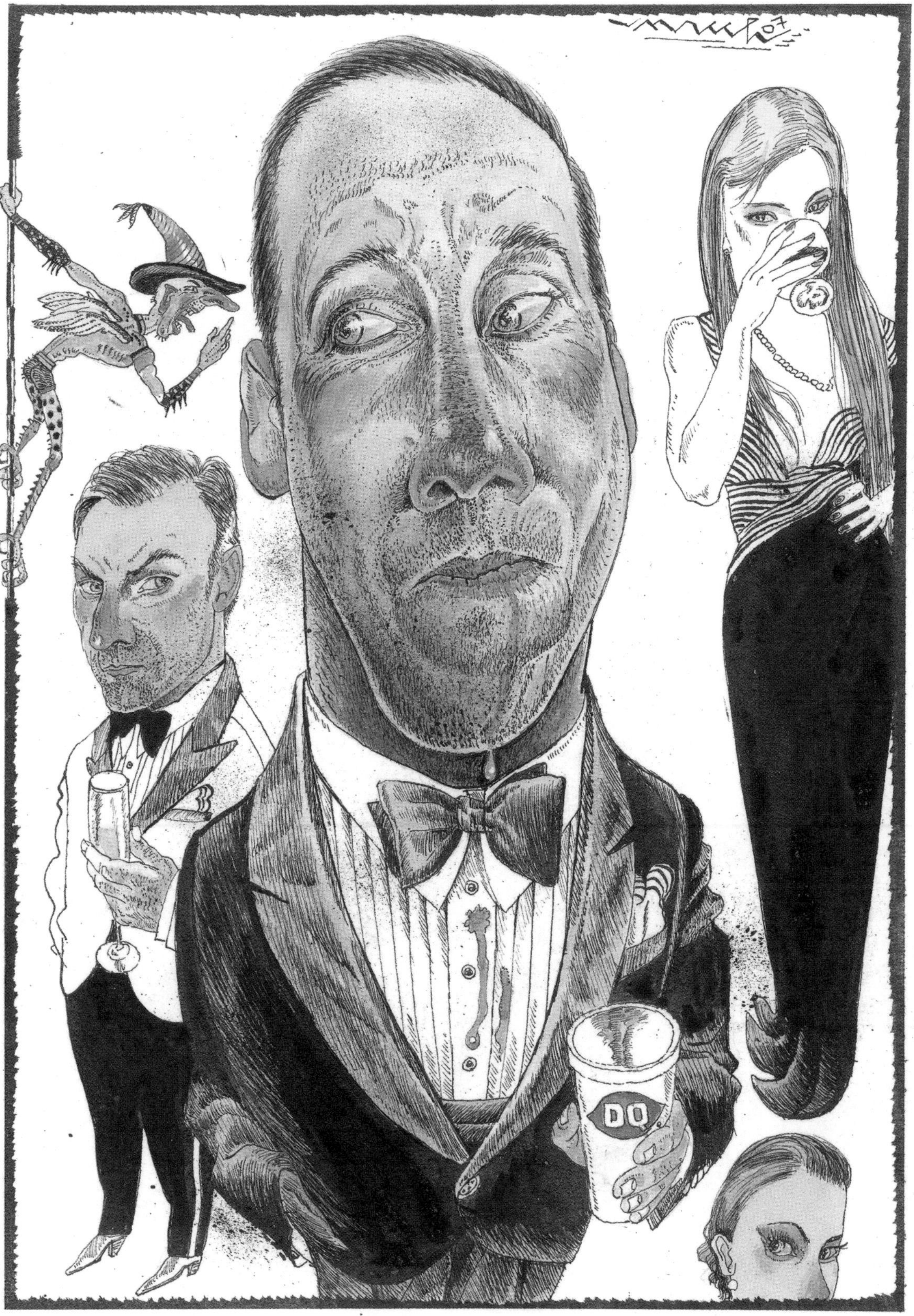
DQ

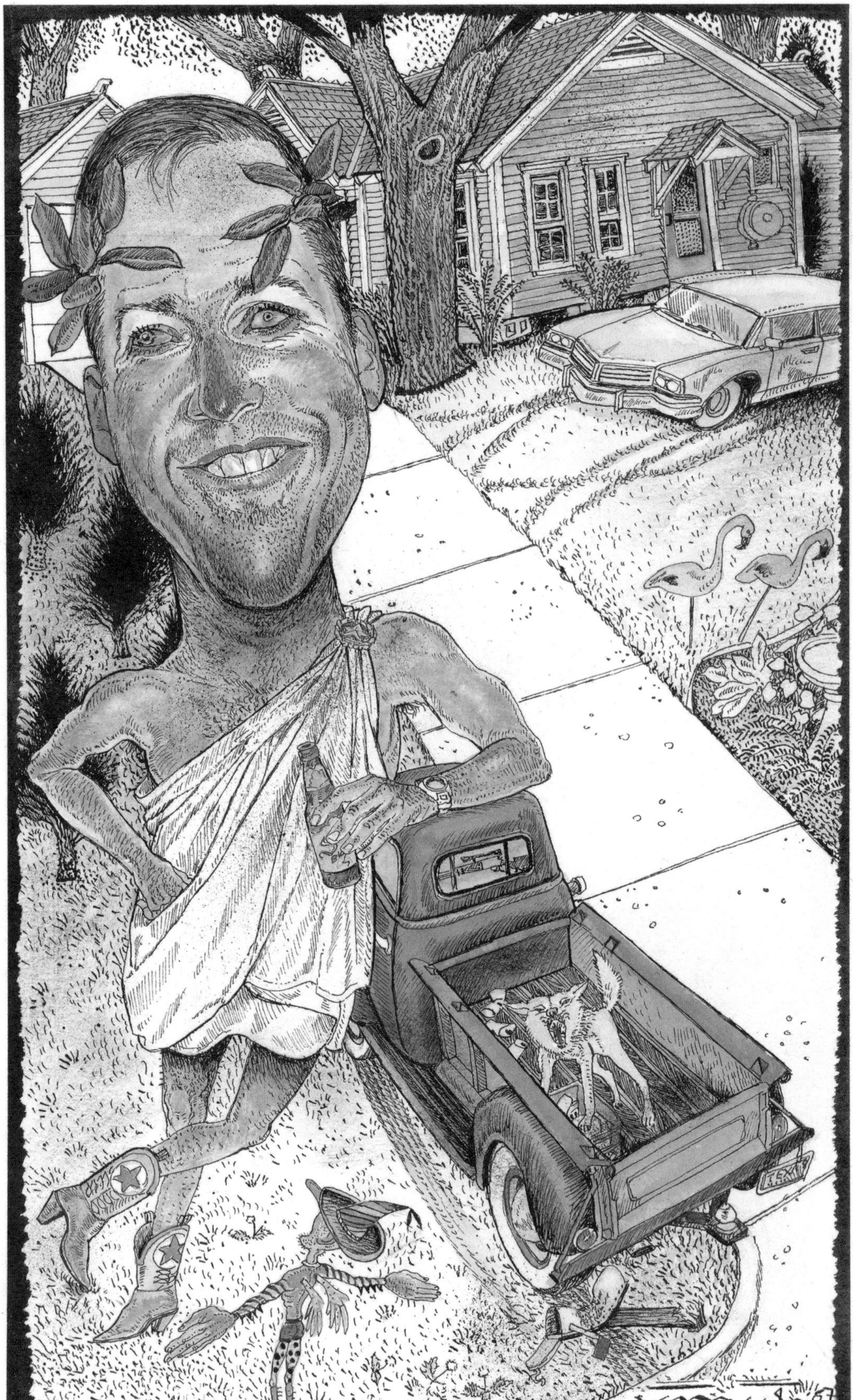

Q: Growing up in Rockwall, I encountered this problem several times: If, when you visit a friend's house, he has parked on his front yard, may you park there too? EMILY MCCLOSKY, AUSTIN

A: The last time anybody parked on the Texanist's front lawn, there followed a quick arrest and a miserable morning spent in the pokey. And although on closer inspection the perp turned out to be an untoward old friend, the Texanist has always maintained that he got what he deserved. A lawn is an outward expression of the pride a person takes in his or her homestead; the degree of its kemptness or unkemptness says a great deal about the creature that serves as its keeper. The Texanist keeps his grass neat, waters by hand, fertilizes twice a year, rakes the leaves in the fall, and broadcasts corn gluten meal as a natural herbicide in the spring.

That said, if your friend's lawn is full of mud holes and strewn with cars, adding your own auto to the ad hoc parking lot will probably not diminish his perception of you in any way. In fact, were you to park on the street, you might run the risk of being thought a priss by this rube of a host. It is always important to observe local customs. The Texanist may take an above-average interest in organic lawn maintenance, but he is no fool. When he finds himself in Rome, he fashions a toga from his bedsheet, guzzles wine from an oversized goblet, and oils himself liberally before a trip to the public baths. Were he to find himself in Rockwall, he would not be disinclined to park wherever the trail might end. ★

Q: A few summers ago I went camping with some girlfriends at Guadalupe River State Park. Imagine our surprise when we were startled one evening by a loudly amorous couple in a neighboring tent. The passionate din went on most of the night. At four in the morning, desperate for sleep, I finally yelled at our horny neighbors, but to no avail. Is it really appropriate to make love in a campground? KATE KISER, AUSTIN

A: The Texanist confesses with apologies that after reading your missive, his first thought was to forward it to Penthouse Forum. His second thought, with another apology, was that this would be the perfect basis for an adult film titled *Guadalupe River State Pork*. His third thought . . . well, the Texanist never thought this would happen to him, but he is having trouble focusing.

As to the question, if you were deprived of sleep and bothered, it was not wrong to cry out. But generally, when happening upon nonindigenous state park fauna in rut, the Texanist responds with applause. Here's to them! Were he to find himself in earshot of the sleeping-bag thrashers whose clamor disturbed you, he likely would have paused in wonderment of the natural world and then vigorously saluted the enthusiastic and impressively protracted doings. Among purveyors of social advice, the Texanist may be alone in his appreciation of campsite copulation; as far as he can tell, no etiquette manuals have addressed this situation. Perhaps one should be written. It might be called *Campground Love: A Many-Splintered Thing*. Or perhaps *The Hornythologist's Guide to the Tented Texas Lovebird*. Or simply *The Kampa Sutra*. ★

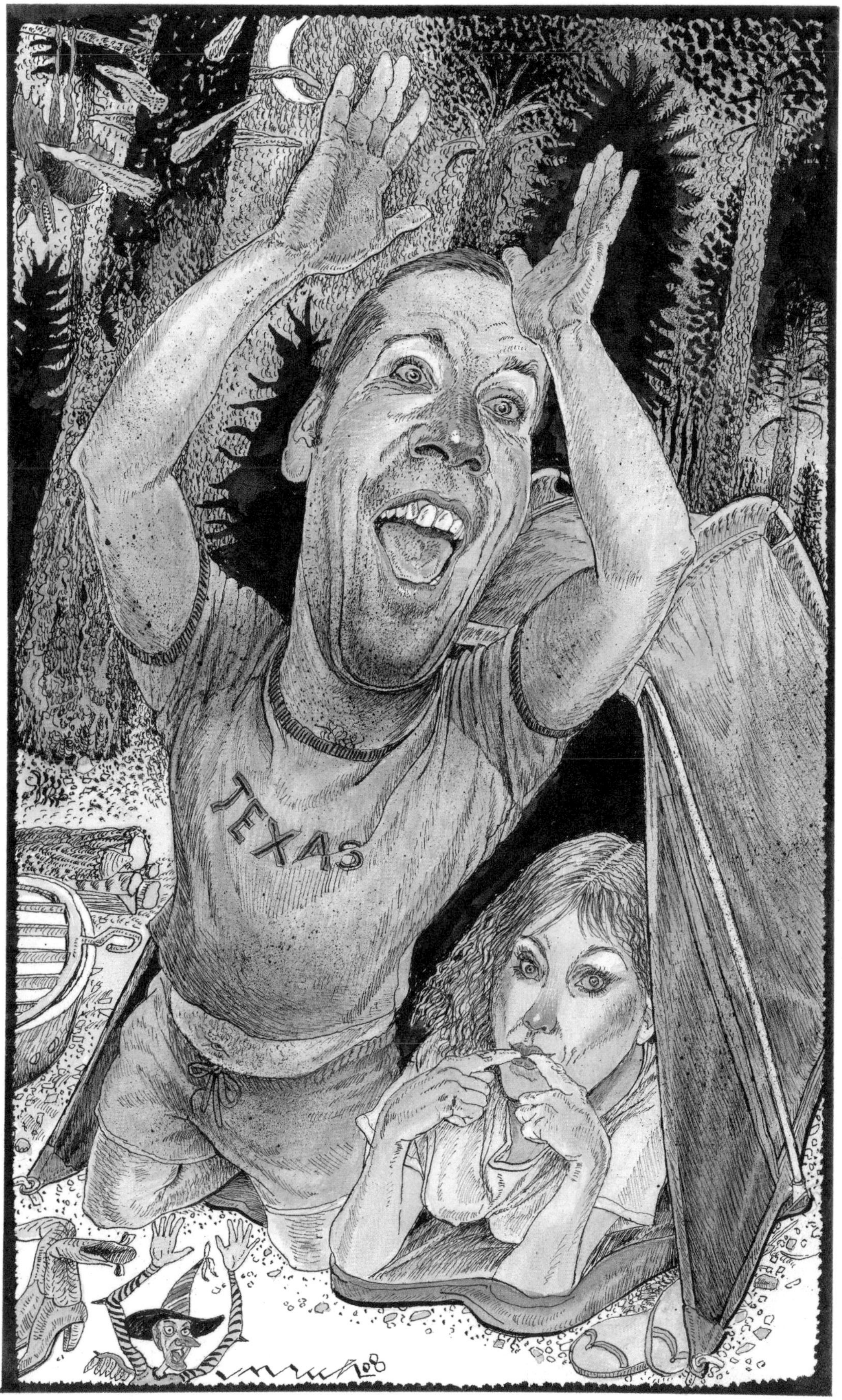
TEXAS

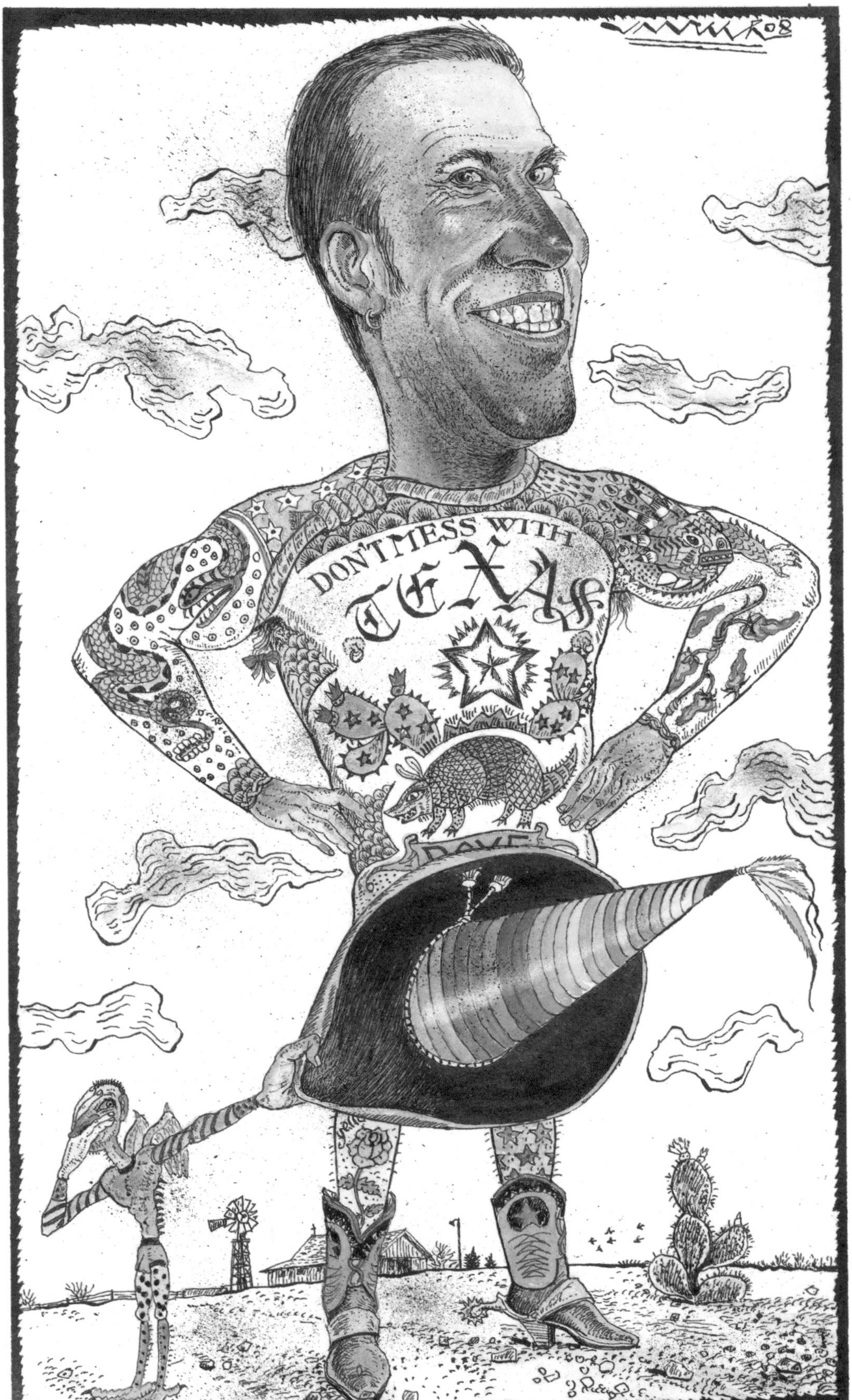
DON'T MESS WITH
TEXAS

Q: Can one have too many Texas tattoos? By Texas tattoo I mean Texas-themed—for instance, a design with half the Texas flag incorporated, the outline of Texas with my Greek letters inside of it, and my newest, a nautical star with the letters T, E, X, A, and S inscribed around the outside, like the star that was on one of our first flags. Just wondering if getting the "Come and Take It" flag might be overkill? JAMES OWENS, LUBBOCK

A: Seeing as how you probably slipped the pesky fetters of propriety a tattoo parlor or so ago, why stop now? At this point, for the Texanist to preach otherwise would be fruitless, as fruitless as informing you now that the nautical star you most recently had permanently inked upon your skin was never featured on any standard of the Republic of Texas but only on a theoretical banner discussed, but never approved, at Washington-on-the-Brazos, known as the Zavala flag after its designer, Lorenzo de Zavala.

But this is not a seventh-grade Texas history class. The Texanist has mined his ample memory banks and concluded that he has yet to encounter the person with too many Texas-themed tattoos. And not being your poor mother, he actually finds the exuberance with which you display your pride in our great state commendable. Honestly, worse choices could certainly be made. The unforgettable sight of a female's unmentionables imprinted with Willie Nelson's bearded mug once elicited a short-lived smile from the Texanist, until it struck him that anytime this lass shared an intimate moment with a gentleman caller, one of our state's most revered icons would be desecrated, repeatedly. That takes it too far. As would the "Come and Take It" tattoo you are considering, if located in the nether territory.

But as you seem to have nothing more than good old-fashioned patriotism and pride on your mind, that place called overkill still lies some untold number of needle pricks down the road. Onward! The Texanist even has a few ideas for your collection: How about a grandiose and detailed depiction of the Battle of the Alamo? Or maybe the Battle of San Jacinto, which, by the way, featured its own very nice battle flag. Better yet, consider the likeness of a grinning Texanist accompanied by one of his most popular sayings: "Come and Take It . . . From the Texanist!" ★

Q: What are the guidelines for male friends helping each other apply sunscreen? I was recently down at the coast with a buddy of mine. My girlfriend wasn't there, so when I was putting on some sunscreen, I asked him if he'd mind doing my back. He nearly had a conniption fit and acted like I had made some sort of depraved request. Did I err? NAME WITHHELD

A: Blessed with a preternaturally bronzed (the fact-checkers say orange) and perpetually glistening (the fact-checkers say unwashed) beach-friendly physique, like that of Hercules film series star Reg Park (who, the fact-checkers say, succumbed to skin cancer in 2007), the Texanist has never himself had much use for sunscreen. His position vis-à-vis ultraviolet radiation shares much with the 43rd president's onetime stance toward Islamic extremism: Bring it on. But he is keenly aware of the medical establishment's point of view regarding the harmful effects of the sun's rays and knows well the strong bonds, but equally strong boundaries, of male friendship. It would be nice if these forces never collided, but male-on-male sunblock application is hardly the only case of fellowship's leading to manly activities that can be misconstrued. Has your friend never hugged a man after a victory in sport? Slapped a man on the buttocks for a job well done? Pinned a man to the floor during a night of drunken Indian leg wrestling that gets a little out of hand? As long as the summer sun shines on Texas's beautiful beaches, men will share shirtless moments frolicking beneath it. If your friend is resolute in his reluctance to "do your back," maybe next time you should bring the girls. ★

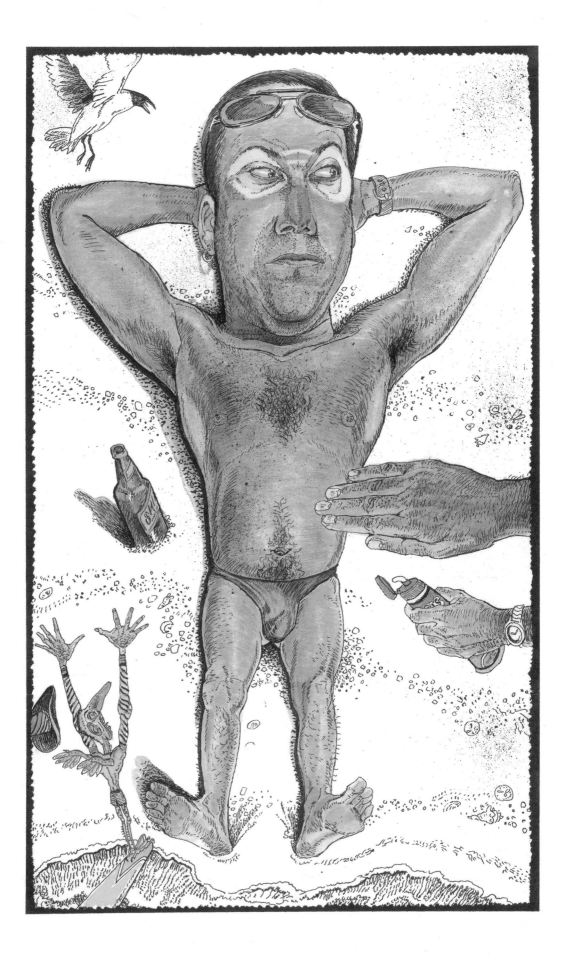

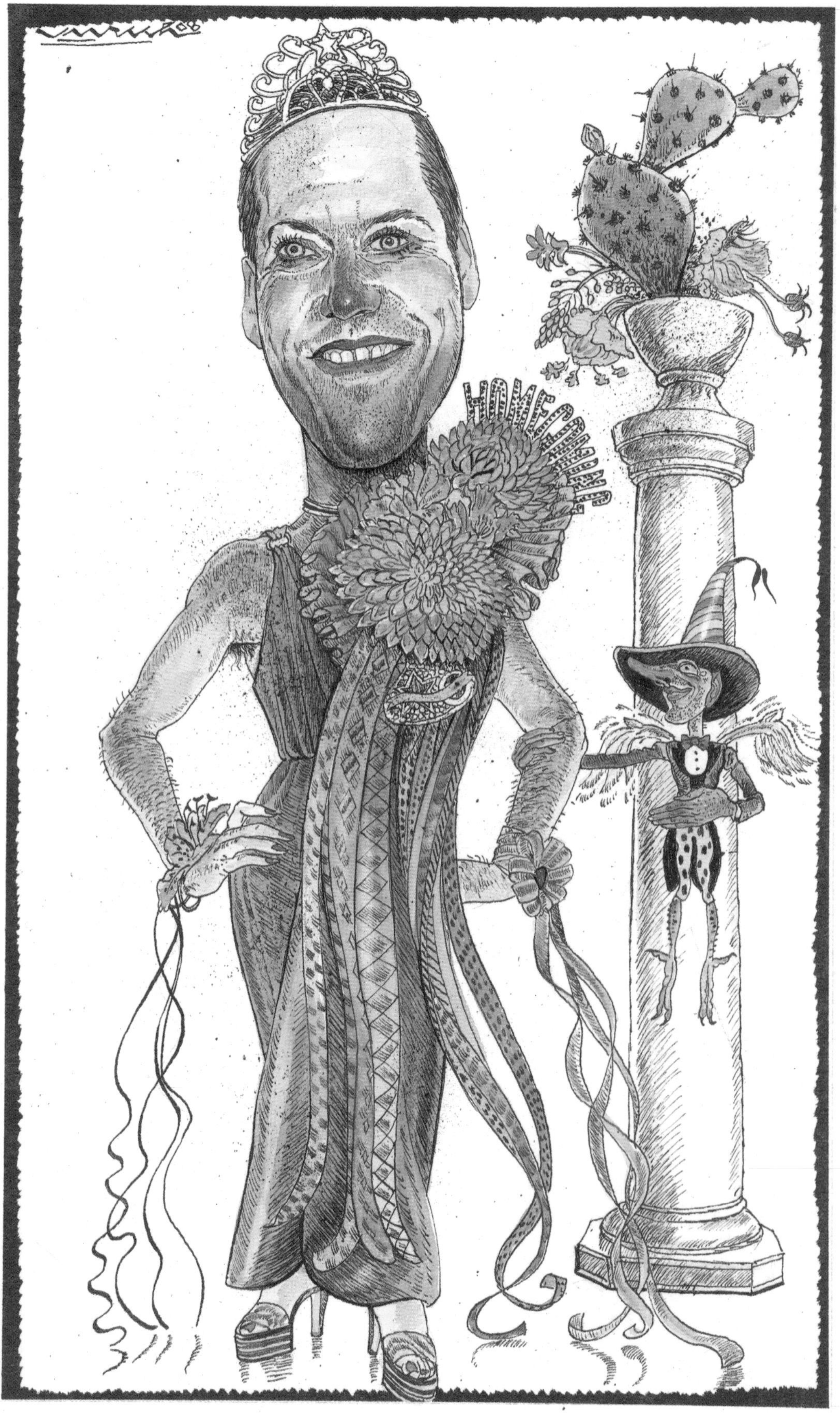
HOMECOMING

Q: My daughter, Kelsey, is a senior in high school this year, and she has never had a boyfriend. When I was in school, I was voted homecoming queen my senior year and received a triple mum. Kelsey has gone mum-less to three homecomings, and I don't want her to have to endure another. Would it be okay for me to buy her one and say it's from a secret admirer?
NAME WITHHELD

A: Looking back on his years at dear old Temple High, the Texanist must confess that his efforts at the time were more often directed toward deflowering than beflowering the female Wildcats skipping past him in the halls. Upon reflection, had he applied himself to the latter, he might possibly have achieved greater success with the former. In those days of yore, the mum, a corsage on steroids, was a worry mainly of the sportarati. Geeks, freaks, tokers, bandos, motorheads, and the Texanist usually had occasion neither to give nor receive the floral trophies. But you have come to the Texanist not for a tale of woe but for affirmation of your plan. And while he is not usually one to abide deceit, he understands that yours is a scheme born of a mother's love. Like a Hallmark card or a sappy made-for-TV movie, you have touched the soft underbelly of the Texanist. Get Kelsey that mum! And make it a double! With all the streamers, teddy bears, bells, and whistles you can afford. As long as she doesn't run with band nerds, goths, religionists, brains, stoners, goat ropers, skaters, rockers, or, God forbid, loners, she won't be totally mortified. ★

Q: How old need a boy be to receive the gift of a first gun?
CHRISTOPHER, AUSTIN

A: Assuming that we are not speaking of some wild-assed hellion with bad intentions, age is neither here nor there. The key to safely arming a young person is found in the guidance provided by the caretaker. If you are willing and able to teach your li'l shooter the finer points of gun use, you may start him early indeed. The Texanist knows whereof he speaks. He has been called a William Tell–cum–Lucas McCain, a modern-day Ad Toepperwein, Annie Oakley reincarnated in britches, and one heckuva shot. Once, he silenced revelers at a cocktail party by extinguishing a candle flame in the host's living room with a Daisy Red Ryder from twenty paces. Many have surmised, as the nimbus of gun smoke cleared from yet another feat of marksmanship, that he must have been born with a gun in his hands. This was not the case. The Texanist, like many a tyke, climbed the firearms ladder—BB (Daisy), pellet (Crosman), .22 (Browning), 20-gauge (Browning)—under his father's cautious tutelage, and therefore has yet to shoot anything (or anybody) he didn't aim to. ★

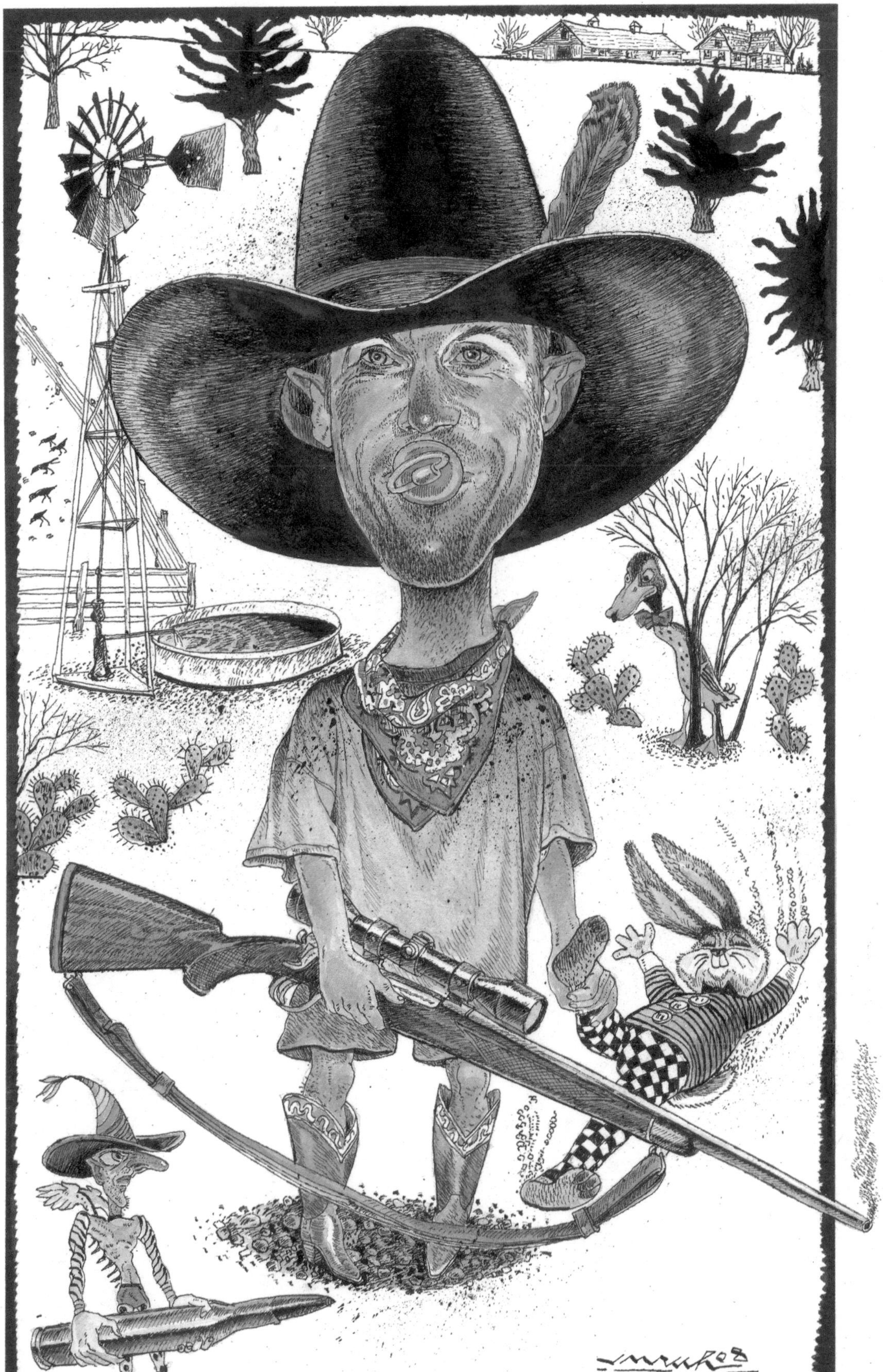

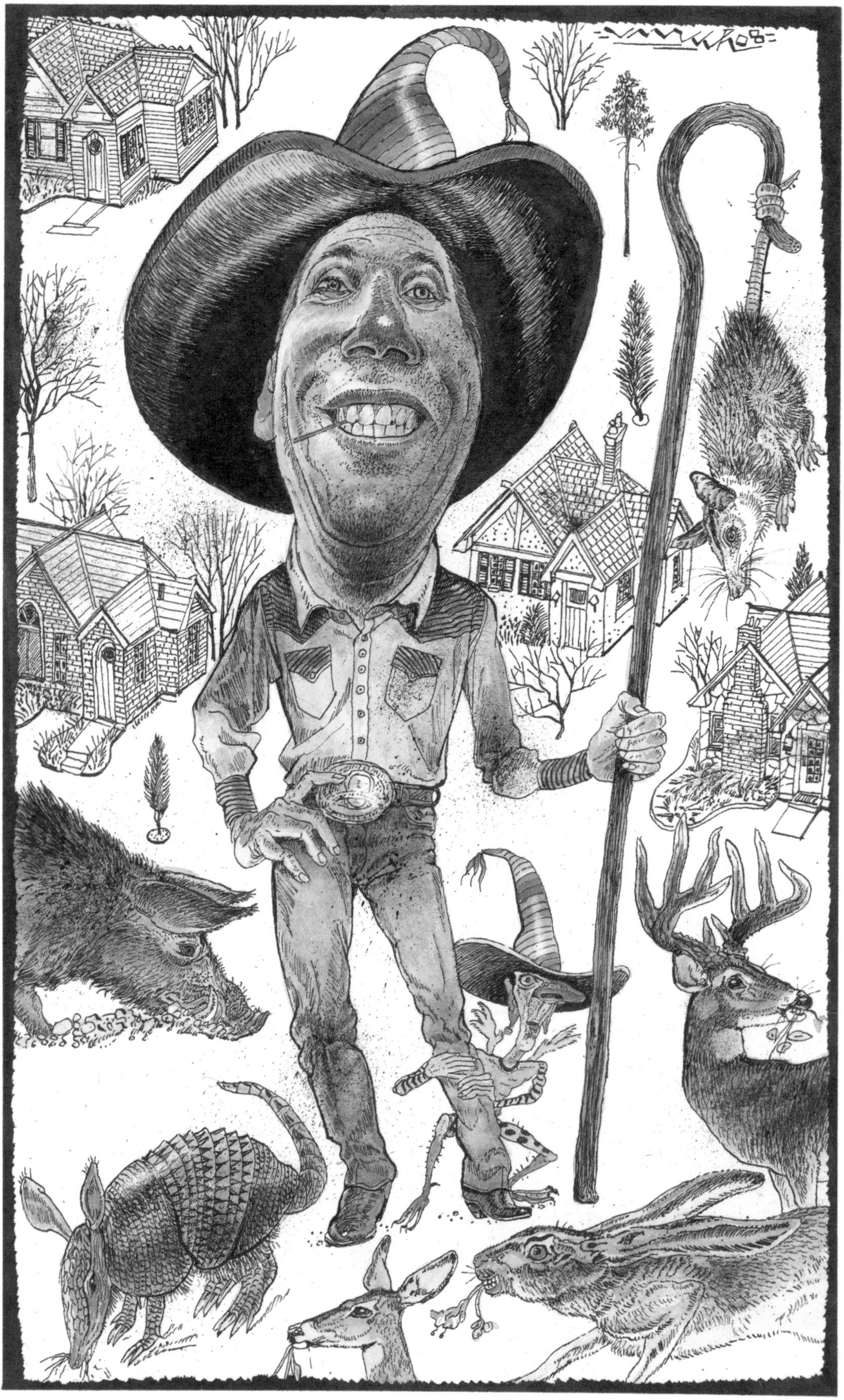

Q: Something has been wrecking my yard during the night and I suspect varmints. I consider myself an animal lover but have reached my wits' end. What can I do to keep them from further destroying my beautiful landscaping? CARLA, BASTROP

A: It may surprise you to learn that the Texanist's coexistence with God's creatures has not been entirely free of occasional violent run-ins with sundry vermin. His fuzzy foes have ranged from beady-eyed squirrels, half-witted white-tails, and yowling feral cats to trash-scrounging raccoons, pale possums, and a bloodthirsty chupacabra. These encounters have tended to be relatively quick and one-sided, though at least one has graduated into a decades-long feud that as of this writing shows no sign of an easy resolution (one day the Texanist will find you, you goat-sucking abomination). But as is often the case, the Texanist would discourage his readers from doing as he does and instead attempt to promote the wisdom of what he says. The plain fact is that in the vast majority of instances your four-legged nocturnal caller is more vagabond than vandal and will, with time, move on to greener pastures (once he's left yours in tatters). If, however, you are as out of patience as you suggest and cannot wait for this to transpire, you may simply peruse the telephone directory and summon your local critter ridder, wildlife relocator, or exterminator. But be warned that we are speaking now of some very cold fellows, men with hollow eyes, hard hearts, and dark, drafty voids where once danced the bright souls of innocent, fauna-friendly children. ★

Q: Every year at wildflower time my wife, whom I love dearly, insists that I come with her and the kids for the annual bluebonnet portrait. I usually protest a little but inevitably end up out there on the side of the road with them. Do I really have to go this year?   NAME WITHHELD

A: The Texanist looks forward with giddy anticipation to wildflower season, when springtime's resplendent splash of *Lupinus texensis* heralds the annual promise (as short-lived or downright empty as it may be) of rejuvenation to the winter wilted. J. Frank Dobie, our great tale-teller and petal-smeller, once declared that no other bloom provides "such upsurging of the spirit and at the same time such restfulness." The Texanist is in agreement. When the full splendor of the bluebonnet's azure blossom is realized across a bucolic landscape, it is a fact that a first-rate photo op is at hand. However, long-held regional tradition dictates that unless one is a toddling child whose button nose is like a magnet to fluttering butterflies, one is not legally required to sit for amateur roadside bluebonnet portraiture. Children are stuck with it, but you, sir, are a grown man and, as such, can make a defensible case for *Lupinus texensis avoidus*. This year, when the time comes, simply be steadfast and mule-like in your refusals. Your spouse's spirit, as Mr. Dobie observed, will upsurge, and a string of profanities, like a garland of roses, will encircle you. Be advised therefore that the blessed restfulness of which Mr. Dobie speaks will evaporate should you choose this course. Yet fear not, as this particular unpleasantness, like the wildflower itself, will in due time subside unto the earth from whence it sprungeth. ★

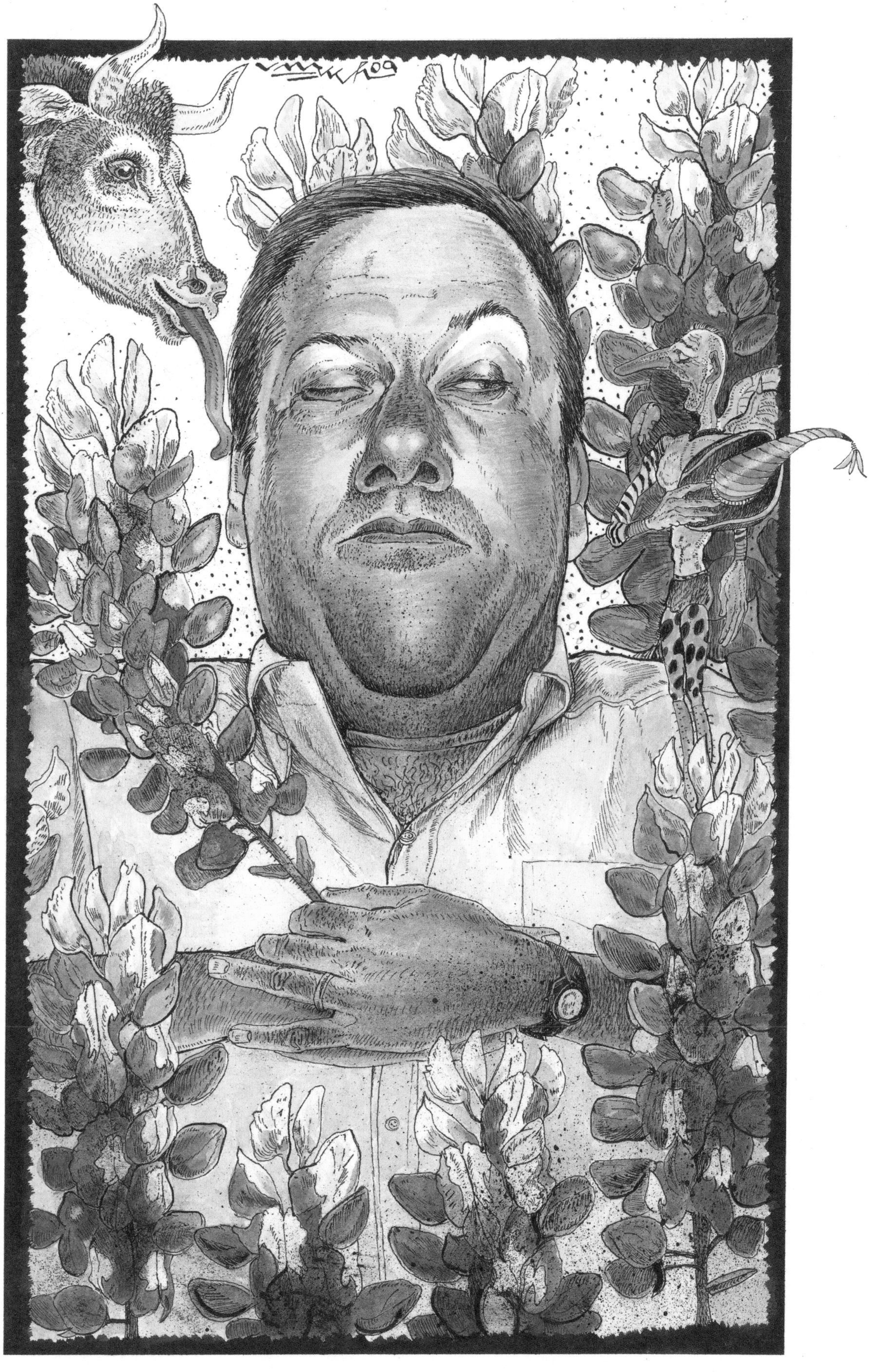

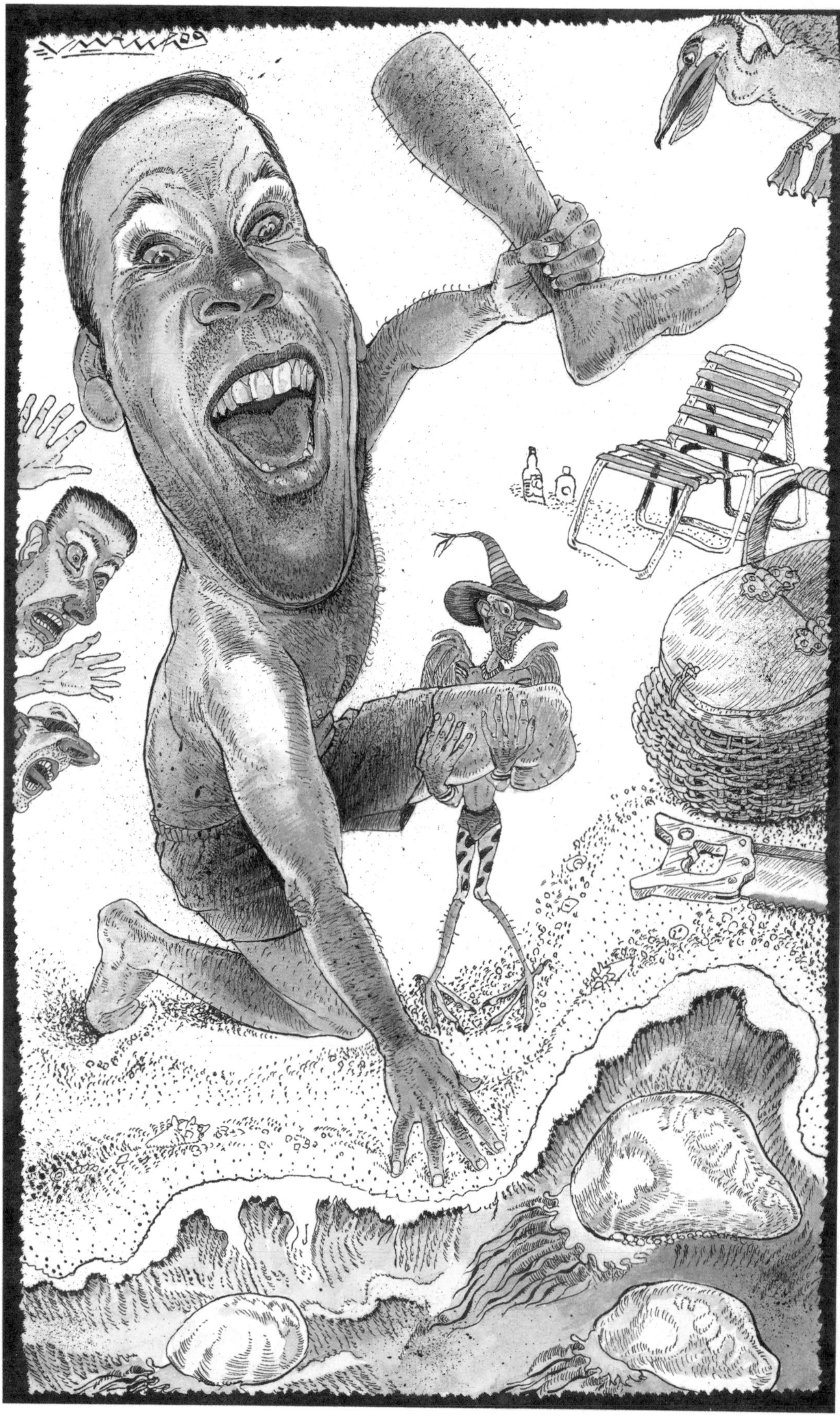

Q: I'm heading down to the beach this Labor Day for the first time ever, and I have heard that the jellyfish can be really bad on the Texas coast. How do you avoid them, and what do you do if you are stung by one?
JUSTIN TORRES, ARLINGTON

A: The Texanist, thank God, has never tangled with any of the three jellyfish most common to the Texas coast. Nor has he endured the venomous lash of the hated Portuguese man-of-war. He does, however, harbor vivid memories of a bloody childhood incident that involved having his bare foot impaled to the hilt by the barbed dorsal spine of a washed up hardhead catfish, but that is a fish tale he'll save for his fish therapist's couch. When beach-going, the Texanist is always coated with a liberal slathering of cocoa butter and always has his full, uncut chest, leg, and back plumage on display (no manscaper he). Perhaps the ample vegetable fat and body hair, like armor, have unintentionally protected him from the medusa's torturous tentacles. The Texanist can't be certain.

The point is that, while blooms of jellies can be abundant along the Texas Riviera, a skin-scalding encounter with one of the stinging gobs of goo need not ruin your getaway. The most important thing is to disregard any "100 percent guaranteed remedy" that involves a list of cockamamy ingredients, including—but not limited to—shaving cream, beer, mayonnaise, tomato juice, and buttermilk. Especially avoid the person insisting on the most persistent of old-wives'-tale-jellyfish-sting remedies: human urine. Even in the face of a red and throbbing leg engulfed from toe to knee in nematocysts, the Texanist would sooner have it sawed off than be peed upon by a chuckling chum. Experts recommend splashing (avoid rubbing) a bit of vinegar on the wound, applying a paste of baking soda or sand, scraping the area clean with a straight edge, and then going back to the vinegar. The Texanist would add that two jiggers of gin, some tonic water, and one quarter of a Mexican lime over ice wouldn't hurt either. ★

Q: Propane or charcoal?

GUS BURNS, CORPUS CHRISTI

A: Over the years, the Texanist has had a foot in both of these combustive camps. Propane is greener, cleaner, and speedier, and on occasion, he has found these qualities persuasive. Charcoal, on the other hand, delivers a slightly better flavor and the pyrotechnical satisfaction derived from setting something on fire. The choice between the two can be said to make manifest the classic struggle between convenience and quality, an ageless battle that has reared its head innumerable times throughout human history. Your query echoes such antique conundrums as "printing press versus illuminated calligraphy," "phonograph versus live band," and "Night Hawk Top Chop't Classic TV dinner versus Momma's home cooking." Needless to say, the Texanist takes this question very seriously. He has studied it at great length, broken it down and built it back up and broken it down again. He has consulted with a wide range of experts in the field of patio cookery, including several semireputable physicists, an ex-volunteer fireman, three trained chefs, and a reclusive cook-off champ. He has burned whole afternoons poring over books in libraries and papers on the Internet. Leaving no stone unturned, he has even taken his inquisition to Academy Sports+Outdoors, a usually fruitless endeavor, which, as usual, produced no fruit. In this particular case, both he and the especially hapless Academician to whom he directed his query were brought to tears as they wrestled, quite literally, with the answer. When later presented with security camera footage that documented how his casual interrogation had gradually turned brusque and irritated until it finally erupted into a full-blown dustup, the Texanist was forced to admit how personally invested he had become in the resolution of your question. Apologies belonged to the Texanist that day, and soon thereafter, at the request of a kindly municipal court judge, he was obliged to trade in his sooty lab coat and firebrand inquisitor's chef hat for the apron of a regular backyard joe. Now he saves the grilling for juicy meats and fresh vegetables. The fact is that a delectable repast can be had with either charcoal or propane, and in lieu of a cook fire of hardwood, either will do just fine. ★

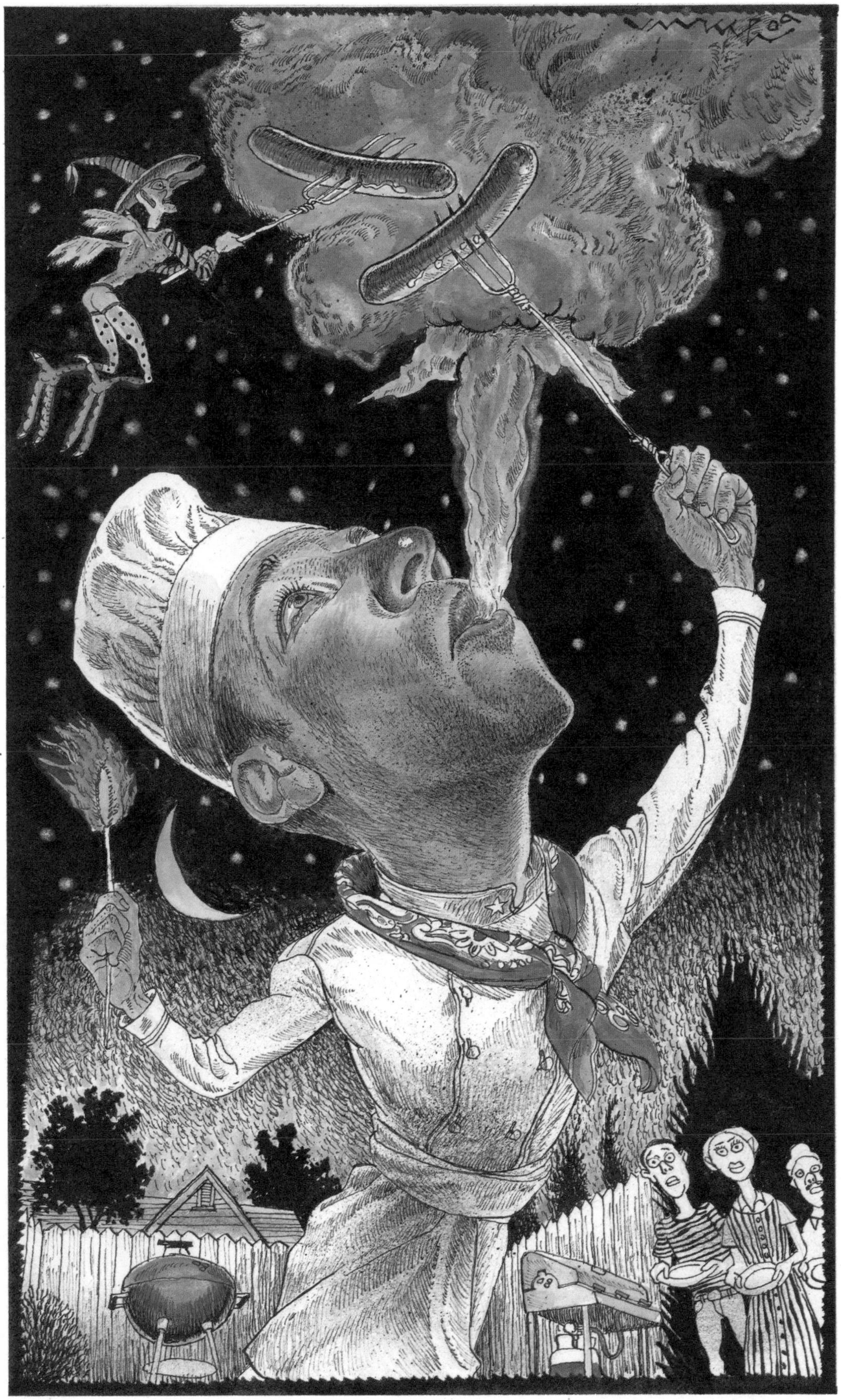

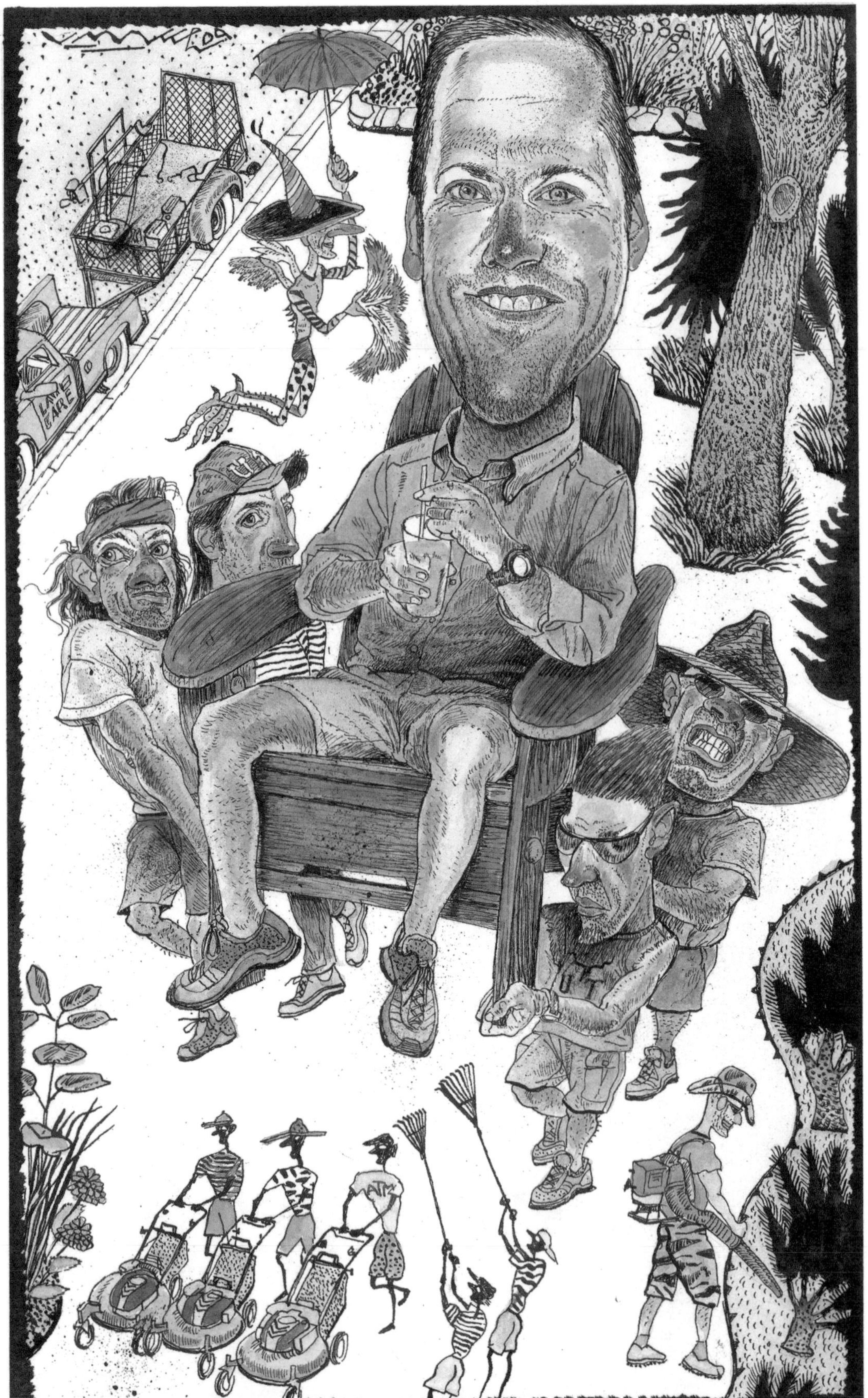
CARE
UT
ATX

Q: Will hiring a lawn service to do my mowing make me soft? **PRESTON CULBERSON, NACOGDOCHES**

A: Well, boy hidy, Mr. Deep Pockets, seems somebody has suddenly found himself standing in some mighty high cotton. And, at the same time, in some increasingly tall grass. Did your numbers hit? Ol' Aunt Hattie, bless her soul, remember you fondly in her will? Well come in? However it happened, you now face one of the classic quandaries of the freshly minted. But it is not so much the softening that comes with newfound wealth that should concern you; in many world cultures such plumpness is a badge of honor. No, what you need to protect is the pride you now take in a job well done by your own hand. For this there is no substitute. Who feeds and waters the patch of God's green earth on which you reside? Who risks life and limb repelling columns of indestructible fire ants and sortie after sortie of dastardly chinch bugs? You do, brave sir. And if you are anything like the Texanist, you do it with a passion that few comprehend. Apocalyptic drought? Hundreds of dollars on leaf bags? A stream of threatening notices from the local water authority? None have kept you from pouring your heart, soul, and previously paltry savings into the shorn seas of verdancy that surround your abode. And when strolling strangers stop to admire your turf while you, filthy and sopping in last night's beer-and-hot-wings sweat, nod proudly from behind 190 cc's of roaring John Deere, it's all worth it, right? The feeling that rushes over a man at that moment is pride. Pride as sweet as the aroma of freshly cut grass in early springtime and as addictive as the fumes from an open gas can. It's clear that you have reached an income level at which domestic help becomes affordable, yet in the case of your landscape, think hard about what you will be giving up. Money can buy many services, but the self-wrought happiness derived from a perfectly mowed lawn carries no price tag. Don't do it. ★

Q: Is it wrong to wear your football team's jersey to church? BILL BLEDSOE, DALLAS

A: The Texanist will endeavor to put the answer to this question in terms that you will understand. As a devoted football fan, you are undoubtedly aware of the phrase "not in my house," a defiant cri de coeur that is generally shouted by a swaggering defensive end who's just sunk a running back for a loss on third-and-short. Well, imagine for a moment that the Almighty is a 265-pound linebacker with meaty arms, a penchant for smashmouthiness, and one of those scary dark visors on His helmet. He who would attend a gathering held in this gentleman's house would do well to observe the accepted dress code or risk the loudest "not in my house" he has ever heard. The proper duds are known as Sunday-go-to-meetings or sometimes even church clothes; an untucked, knee-length football jersey may be considered acceptable and even quite sporty in certain arenas, but not in God's house. The Texanist is sincerely shocked by how suddenly the sartorial sands seem to have shifted. It wasn't all that long ago that Tom Landry could be found patrolling the sidelines in jacket, tie, and trademark fedora. And this was after church. Nowadays jackets, ties, fedoras, and all garments not league sanctioned are forbidden on the sidelines. Forbidden. Although the Texanist, who is himself a high-spirited soul, applauds the gusto with which you aim to express your boosterism, he would have you suit up for church and save the jersey for the post-worship Barcalounger. ★

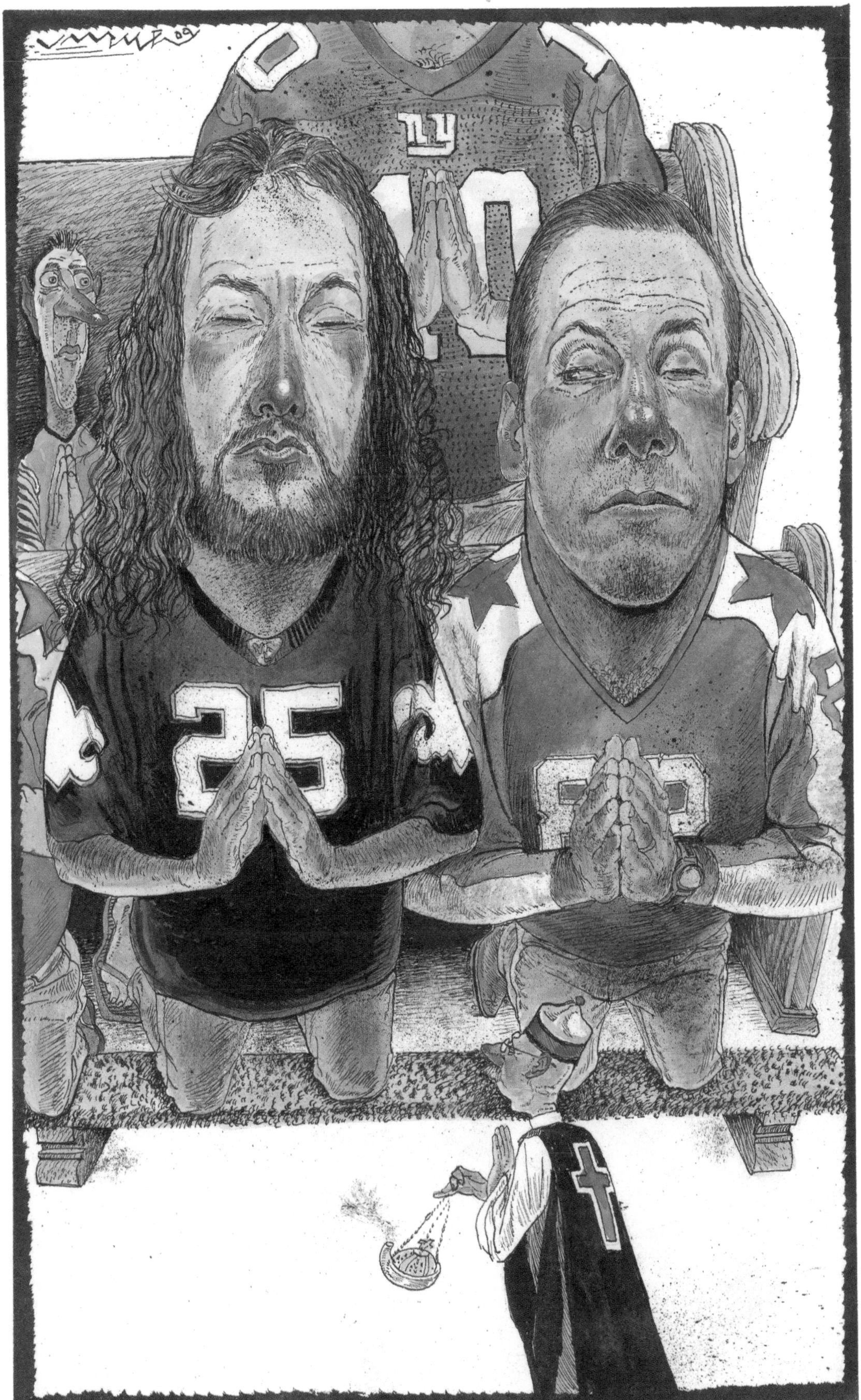

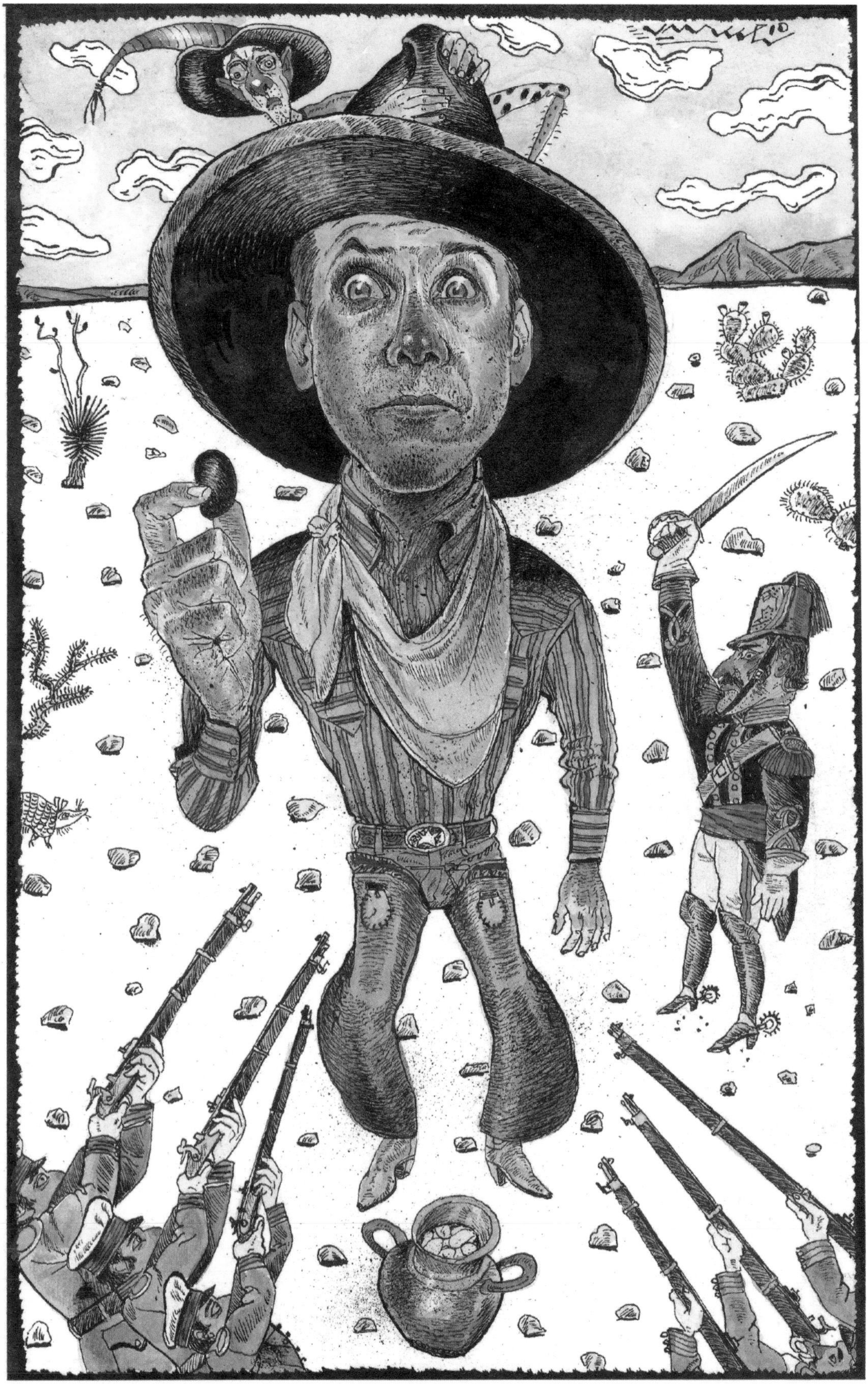

Q: I'm perplexed about the recent black bean craze. Growing up, we had refried, pinto, or ranch beans with our Mexican food, but now it seems everyone is flocking to the black bean. Maybe it's my thoughts about the Mier Expedition, when the captured Texans had to draw beans out of a pot and the ones drawing black beans were shot. Is it real Tex-Mex if it is served with a black bean? ED BLAIR, DALLAS

A: The Texanist's love affair with beans is such that when faced with accusations that he is full of them, he has at times been incapable of denying it with a straight face. Those who have witnessed him reach level fourteen of his famous fourteen-layer bean dip with a single scoop can attest to this passion for bean consumption. But you are right, platters of so-called Tex-Mex that feature black beans instead of pintos do seem to occur more than they once did. In the Texanist's recollection, neither El Chico nor El Chacho, the two Tex-Mex eateries most frequented in his Temple youth, offered anything even resembling *el frijol negro*, although his focus then would have been on the baskets of glistening sopaipillas, an official pastry of Texas. So too are you right, or at least not wrong, to question the provenance of black bean–sided entrées. Generally, authentic Tex-Mex is distinguishable by its muted colors, with shades of yellowy orange and brown dominating the plate. Dishes that have origins in Mexico's interior regions come with more contrast—bright sauces, stark-white rice, and beans of ebony. As for the latter's gaining on the former in popularity, you can thank a population with an evolving palate. Black beans are also thought to be more healthful than pintos, though, as you point out, this has not always been the case. Having a preference for either is fine, but connecting an aversion to a particular bean with an infamous chapter in the history of the Republic of Texas is, in the Texanist's mind, a stretch. In those unfortunate doings of March 25, 1843, referred to by the chroniclers of such events as the Black Bean Episode, the selection of a black bean meant death. Today that same bean choice will not carry with it an outcome so dire. ★

Q: I want to be a Texas rancher. Currently I'm a mechanical engineer (raised in San Antonio). How do I break into ranching? ANN MORTON, CHICAGO

A: The desire to sit back down at the old drawing board of life and sketch up new blueprints is not uncommon and can occasionally result in pleasant renovations. Charles Goodnight, before he broke into ranching, spent time as a racehorse jockey in Port Sullivan. Willie Nelson sold vacuum cleaners door-to-door. The Texanist, until very recently, didn't even have a job and would spend the "workday" drinking beer in his underwear, sometimes at the bar. But while the grass on the other side of the fence can at times appear lush, verdant, and indeed quite suitable for grazing livestock, you must remember that under the harsh Texas sun that green grass can quickly yellow and may even turn to dust and blow away completely (plus the fence will inevitably require mending). The rugged and bucolic imagery of the ranching life has always been alluring, but you would do well to consider the realities. Before trading your compass, slide rule, and pocket protector for a horse, a branding iron, and a chance to be called "tenderfoot" down at the feed store, the Texanist suggests you test the waters (assuming there are any). Sign up for the Longhorn cattle drive at Big Bend Ranch State Park or, better, spend a summer sabbatical working on a South Texas spread. Steer clear of the posh dude ranches, which only serve to perpetuate the myth that the cowboy's life is all about freedom, chuck wagons, and Jew's harps. Whether you're dealing with cattle, sheep, goats, or miniature donkeys, you'll find that ranching is hard, dirty work. It is also much smellier than being a Chicago mechanical engineer. Especially if you're dealing with the tiny donkeys. ★

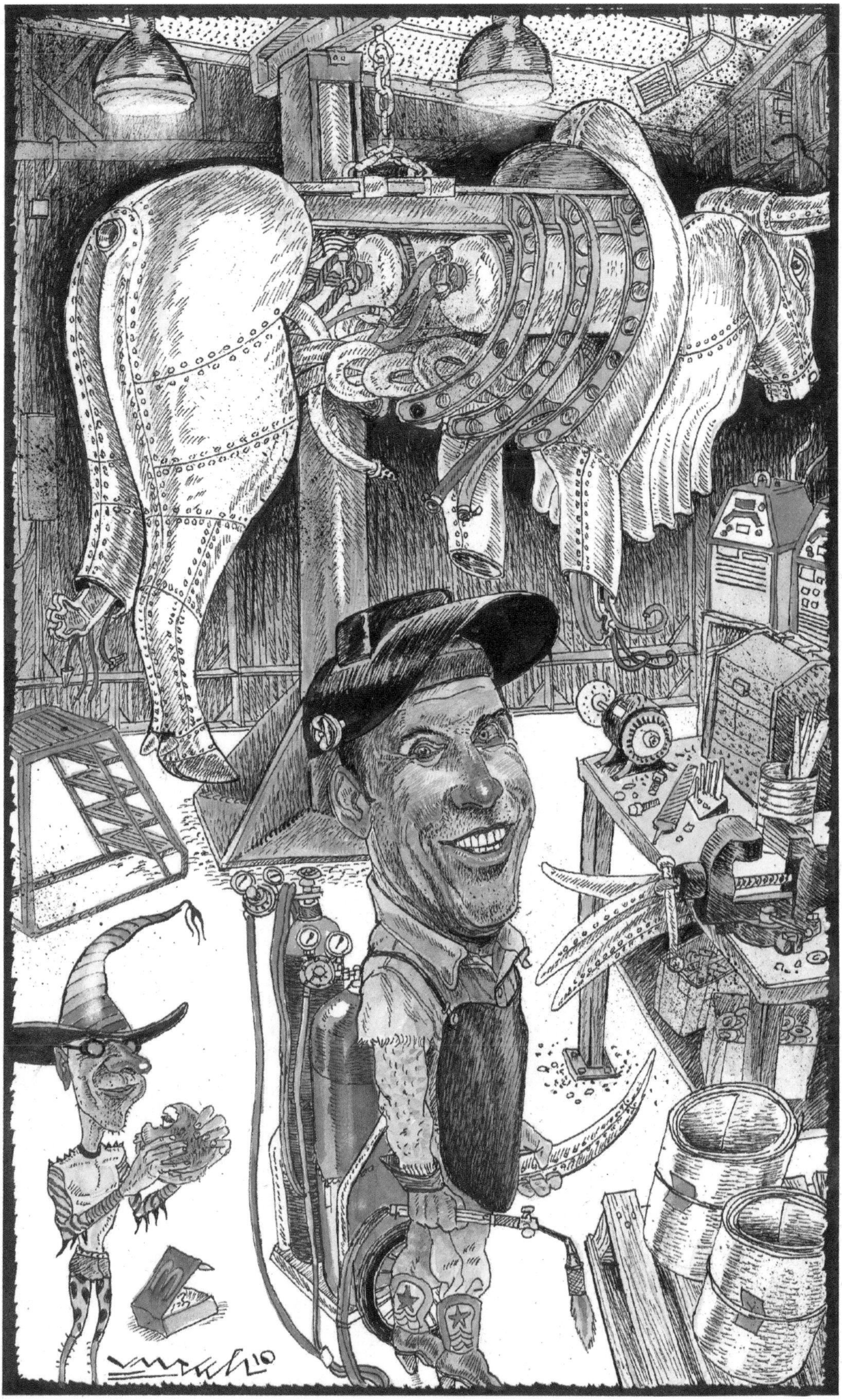

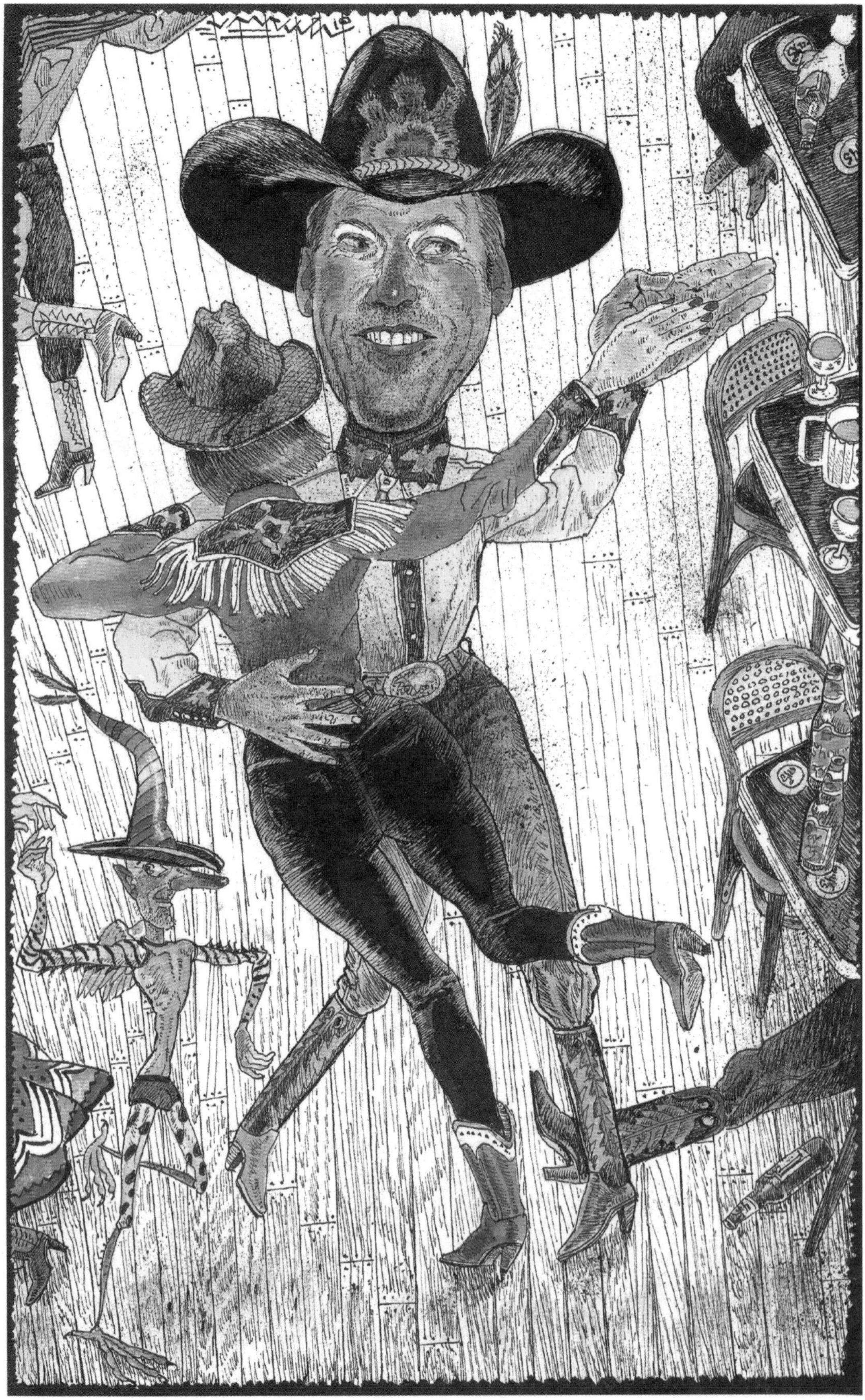

Q: My husband and I go dancing almost every weekend, but I end up dancing with his best buddy more than I do with him. His friend is just a better dancer, and there's no hanky-panky going on but I'm starting to feel guilty. Do I need to stick with the one that brung me? NAME WITHHELD

A: The conventional wisdom would have you reserve your dance card for him that brung you, yes, but the conventional wisdom would also have you stop at five tequilas and refrain from trying to "sit in" with the band as guest vocalist on the "Cotton-Eyed Joe." Where's the fun in that? The Texanist learned how to navigate a dance floor from overbearing junior cotillion chaperones at the Knights of Columbus hall in Temple. (Another flaw in the conventional wisdom: Back then the one that brung you was often your mom.) These ladies instilled in him a firm conviction that dance cards are made to be filled. And if it requires the efforts of multiple partners to fill yours, you should not feel ashamed. The real question is not whether you must dance only with the one that brung you but why the one that brung you didn't also brung his dancing shoes. If it's because he would rather drink beer to excess and dribble tobacco spit down his chin and onto the crisp white Western shirt you gave him for Christmas, then he has only brung the situation on himself and you should not feel guilty. ★

Q: On a recent family vacation my son asked from the backseat what was being cultivated in all the fields we were passing. I hadn't the faintest idea, but I told him it was wheat. How bad was this lie? And what exactly is growing in those South Texas fields? BOB TALBOT, ARLINGTON

A: Welcome to the Texanist's world. His keep is earned by way of handling inquiries such as these. In fact, he sometimes likes to imagine, when staring at another bulging mailbag, that he is merely driving down the highway of life while readers lob questions "from the backseat." And though as a rule he responds to his inquisitors with the strictest fidelity to verifiable data, he is well-aware that questions from the actual backseat of a moving car have been answered improvisationally and with only casual attention to the truth since before there was a backseat. Or a car. Or even a paved highway. As in your case, the inquisitors are more often than not hypercurious offspring bent on getting immediate answers to the obscurest of mysteries. "Who invented mustard?" "Can chocolate go to heaven?" "Do butterflies poop?" "Why is that policeman chasing us?" "Aren't you going to stop?" "Will I be able to visit you at the penitentiary?" Et cetera, et cetera, ad infinitum. The important thing to keep in mind is that when the subject matter concerns roadside attractions, there are very few recourses to which a skeptical child may turn, since by the time the question has been fielded and the reply considered, the curious crop or machinery or mime troupe has already been left far behind. So go ahead, have some fun. In truth, those fields might have been planted with anything. From alfalfa to zoysia, if it grows under the sun, it likely grows in Texas. Wheat? Why not? It could have been wheat. It could have also been gum stalks, doughnut vines, or orange juice grass. When the truth is available, it is generally advisable to use it, but in its absence there is little harm to be found in employing the improvisational arts, so long as you are doing 65 down an open road. Buckle up and drive friendly. ★

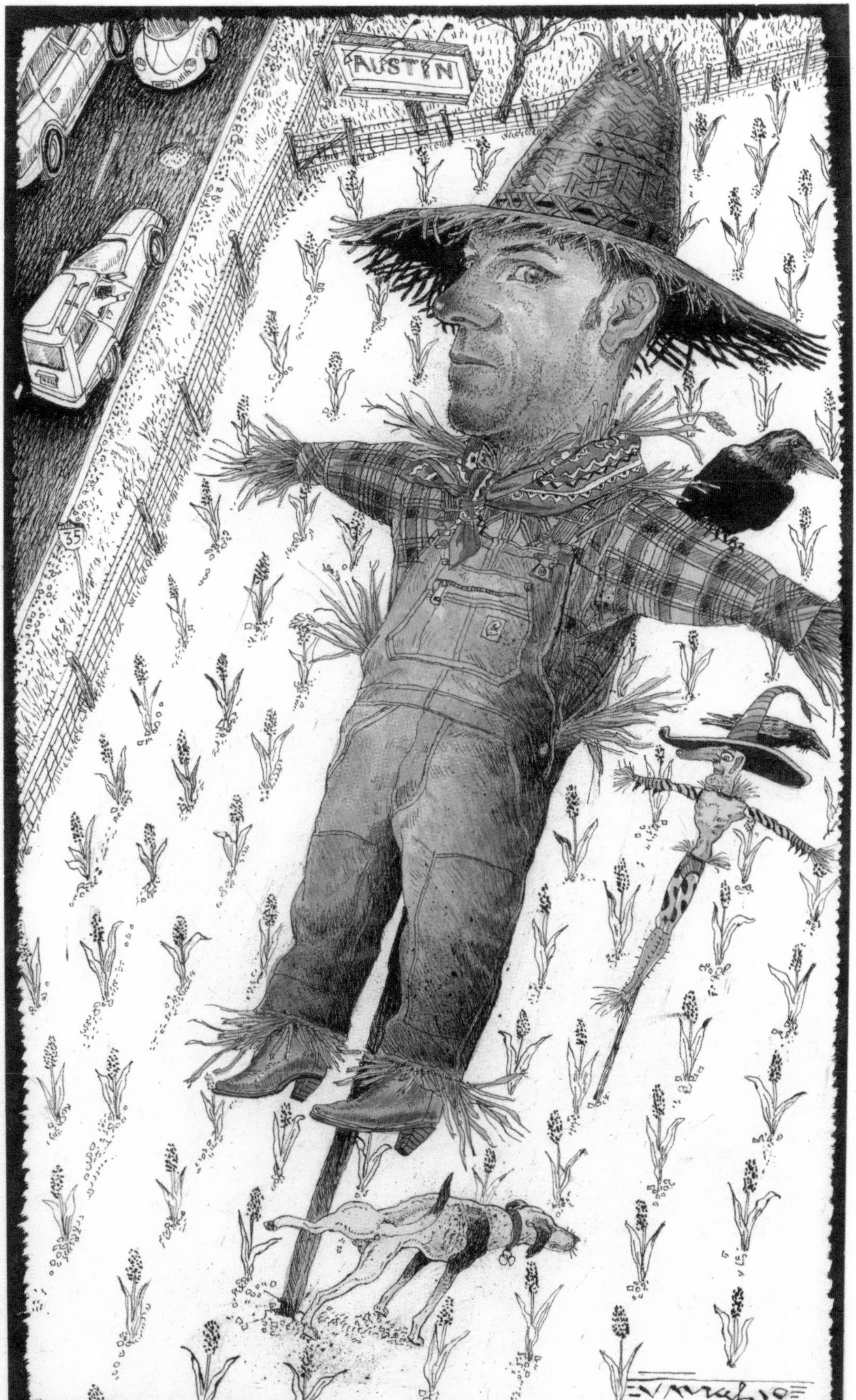
AUSTIN
35

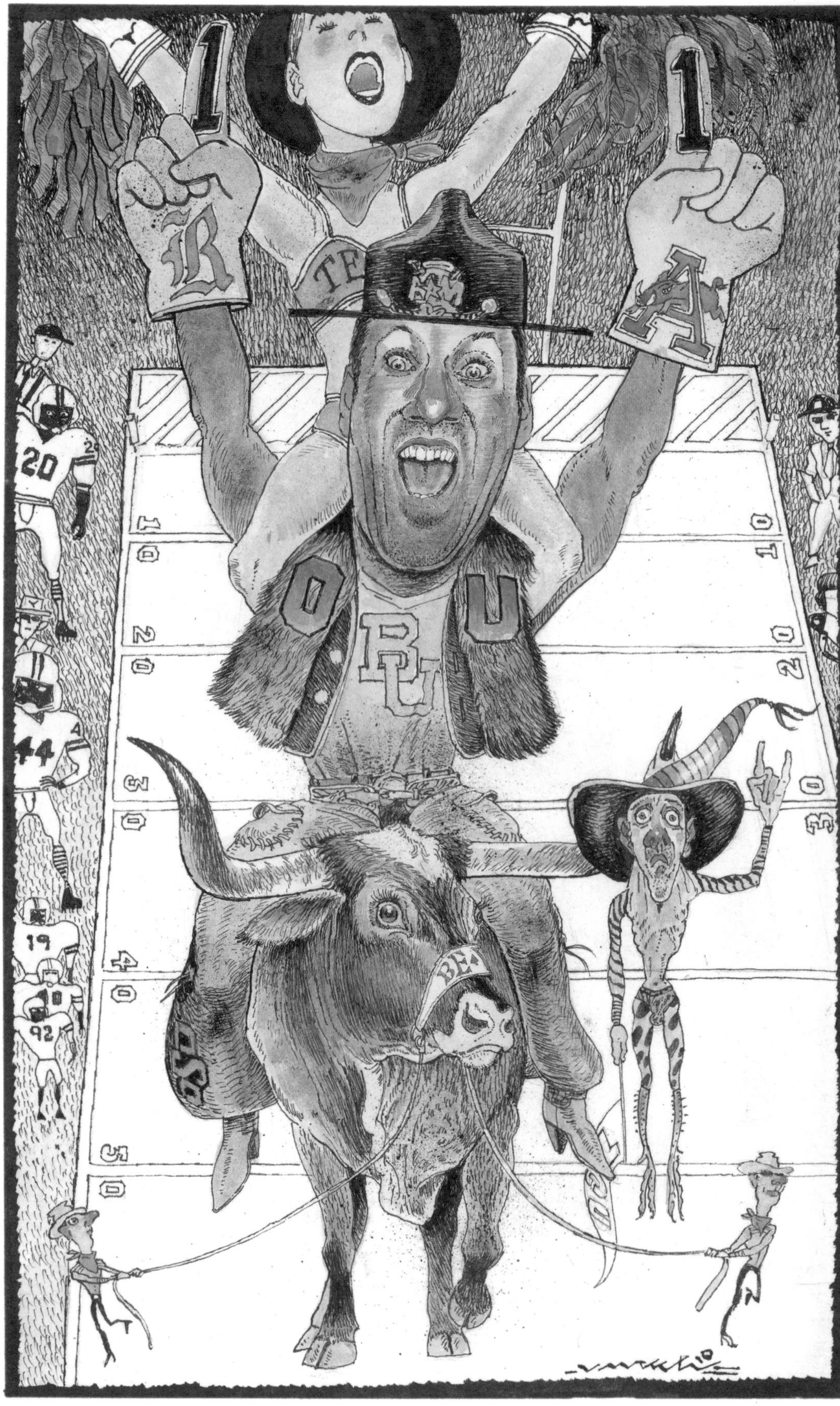

1
1
R
A
TE
O U
ORU
20
44
19
92
10
20
30
40
50
BE
OSU

Q: I wear the colors and symbols of a university I never attended because I admire its history and traditions. Does this make me as stupid as the people who wear burnt orange simply because UT has a big marketing program?
JOHN DULL, PASADENA

A: Clothes make the man, whether you choose to cover your naked body with jeans and a plain white T-shirt or the pin-striped suit of a big-city banker. (A corollary: In the Texanist's experience, there are certain situations where a lack of clothes can also make the man, but it is absolutely critical to properly judge when you are in these situations and not in another type of situation where a lack of clothes only makes the man have to write letters of apology to all the people in his wife's extended family.) Along the spectrum of sartorial significance (at one end lie the myriad uniforms of our military; at the other, a pair of plain blue swimming trunks), a piece of clothing adorned with school colors and symbols falls somewhere between the jersey of a professional sports team and the tank top of a bygone political campaign. Be the wearer a card-carrying ex-student association member or a nonattending booster such as yourself, he is required to sport that garment with purpose. Donning a school's colors (or a "Save the Whales" T-shirt) effectively deputizes you as an emissary of that institution (or cause) and means that you must possess reverence for—or at least some vague awareness of—its storied traditions, current win-loss record, and ranking in the coaches poll. Nothing is more depressing than striking up a urinal conversation with a man wearing the ball cap of your alma mater only to discover, after an unhinged, ten-minute rant about the special-teams coach, that this man did not attend your school, is wearing the hat only because his wife's brother left it in his car, and couldn't care less. As long as you are mindful not to become this man, Mr. Dull, it is fine to wear whatever you like. ★

Q: How many Gulf oysters does it take for a person to see results from the aphrodisiac qualities that they are said to possess? My wife and I were recently visiting Galveston and shared three dozen to no avail.
NAME WITHHELD

A: Ah, the oyster. The most delectable and voluptuous of all the sea's fruits, supple and salty, posed there on the half shell like Aphrodite herself. The Texanist has been known to wantonly lap up piles of these lovelies in sessions that last for hours, and although the purpose of such binges has been more epicurean than erotic, he has not failed to take notice of the effect a boatload of bivalves has on his libido. And, truth be told, the results have ranged from "Katy, bar the door" to "Katy, not tonight, the Texanist doesn't feel so good." See, the thing they don't tell you about oysters—or cobra blood, powdered rhinoceros horn, Spanish fly, tiger penis, barbecued beef ribs, skink flesh, wolf meat, and all the other ingestibles said to possess aphrodisiacal qualities—is that eating an amount sufficient to produce the desired effect may also leave you feeling too full to perform (such is the case, at least, with tiger penis—very hard to digest). Another thing they don't tell you is that any uptick in sexual desire that appears to correlate to the "love potion" is actually derived from the eater's openness to and hunger for such an uptick in the first place. And it is clear, to the Texanist at least, that on the evening in question you were simply not "in the mood" for an uptick at all. Which happens. Surely Mrs. Name Withheld understands that these are mollusks, not miracles. But you shouldn't get your dauber down. The night wasn't a total loss, after all, as you were able to enjoy 36 of Galveston Bay's finest, probably chased down by a few cold beers, and catch all of *The Tonight Show* to boot. What could possibly be better than that? ★

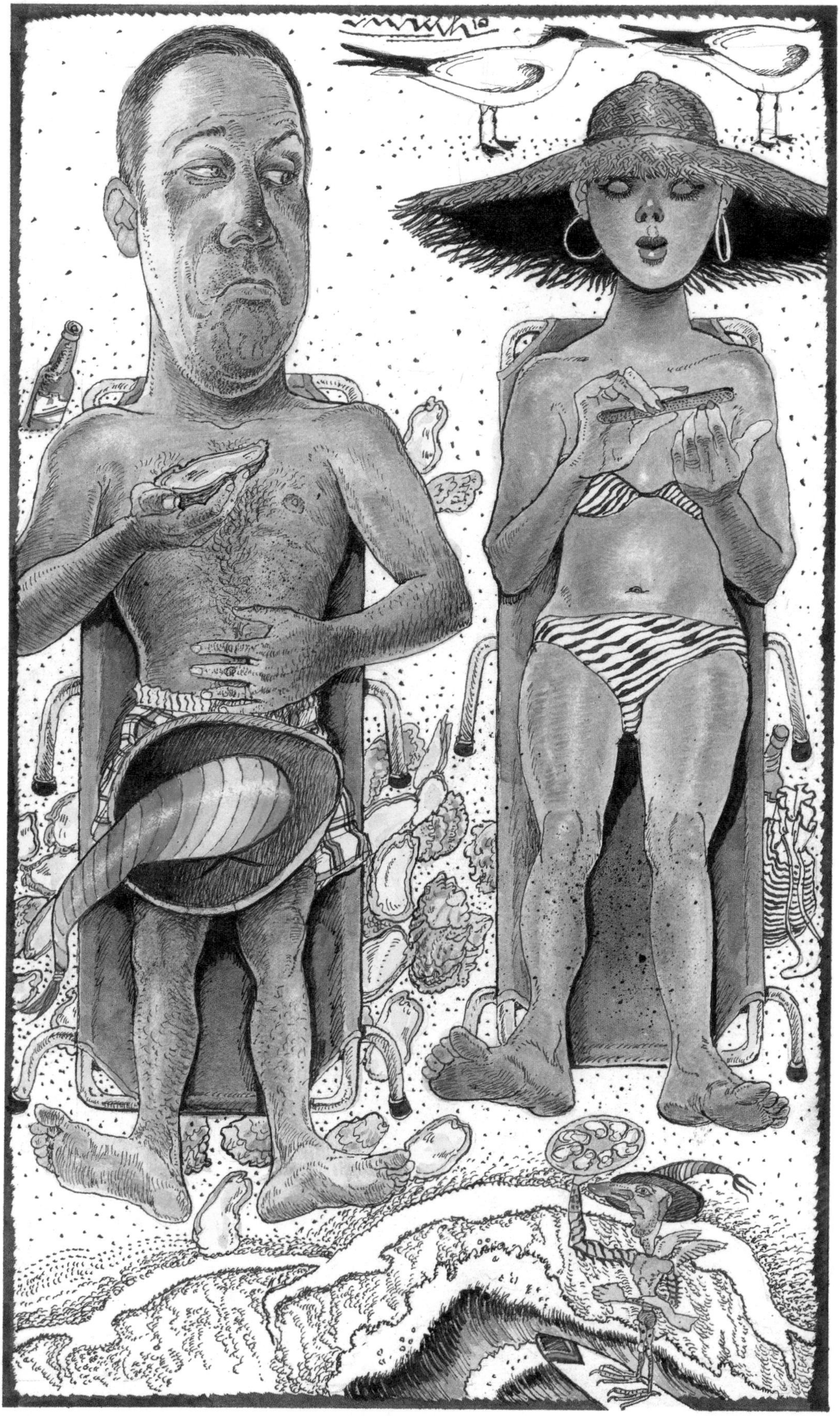

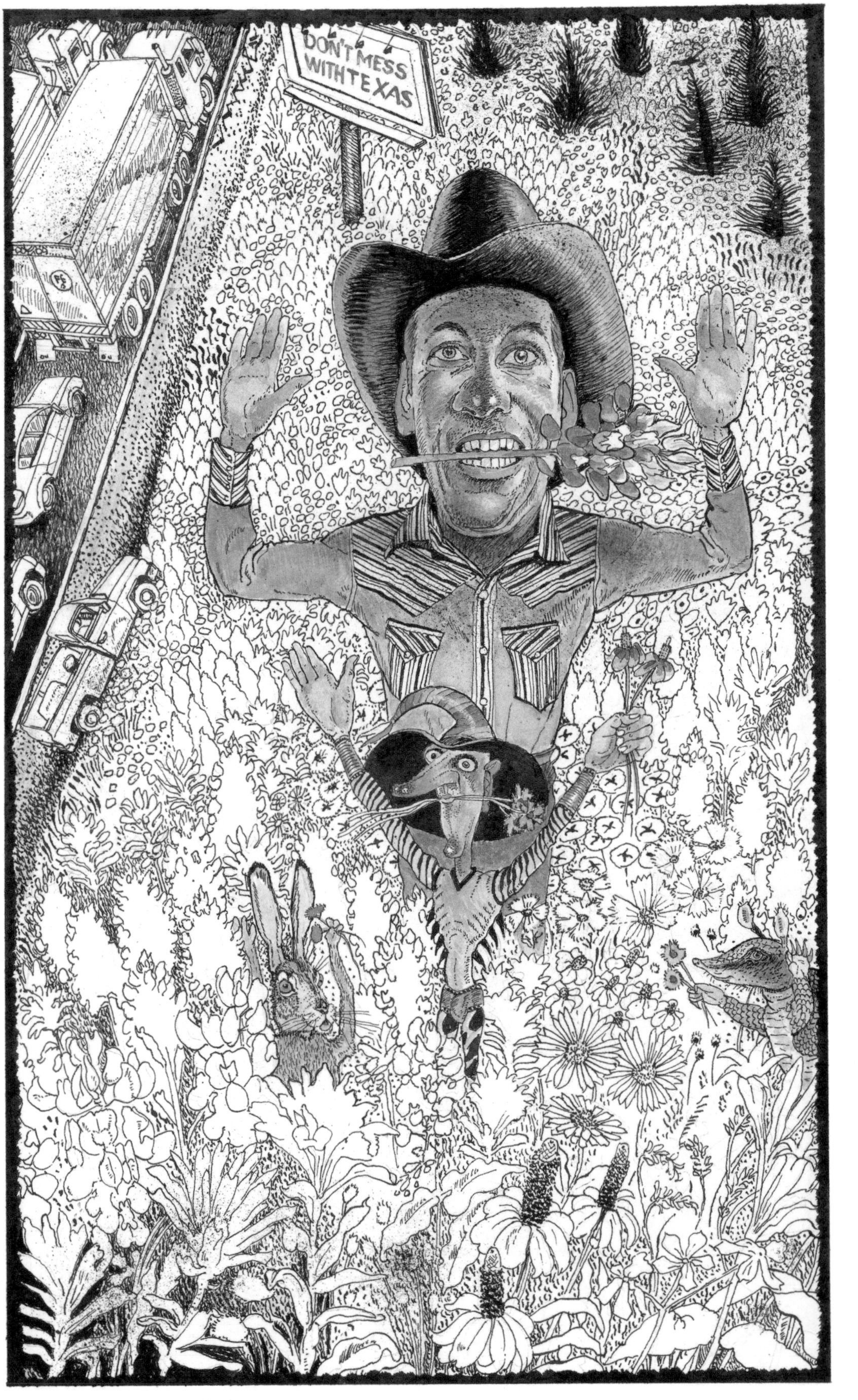
DON'T MESS
WITH TEXAS

Q: I was wondering if you could explain proper bluebonnet protocol. I was always taught not to pick any bluebonnets, because they belonged to Texas. Is this true? LINDSEY BACON BERTRAND, COLLEGE STATION

A: Texas is crisscrossed by more miles of public roadways than any other state in the union, and from the time these scenic byways were first blazed through the wilderness, our ingenious forebears have been toiling, often in obscurity, to ensure that there would be a sufficient number of attractions along them. It is thanks to the efforts of these pioneers that we have so many spots at which to pull over and snap photos, worthy locales like the Cadillac Ranch, in Amarillo; the Beer Can House, in Houston; the Leaning Water Tower, of Groom; the former World's Largest Pecan, in Seguin; and Pancho Villa's mummified trigger finger, in El Paso, to name just a few. But the works of man, sublime though they may be, will always pale in comparison with the annual blossoming of bluebonnets. *Lupinus texensis*—as she is known to, well, nobody—is, along with four other lupines, the state flower, and as such she does belong to Texas, but only in the sense that enchiladas and the music of Bob Wills do. No statute on the books prevents you from plucking a bouquet from the public medians and shoulders alongside our highways (as for flowers growing on private property, the Texanist assumes you need not ask that question). Yet even though the uprooting of one of these blossoms will not result, as many children are taught, in the sudden arrival of an angry posse of Texas Rangers, come to drag you off by your ear and toss you in the hoosegow, you should nonetheless refrain. While not officially outlawed, the act of pulling up a bluebonnet remains a Texas taboo of the highest order, worse than even vegetarianism or rooting for the Redskins. Proper protocol is simple: Leave the flowers in the state in which they were found, which is to say, unpicked. ⋆

Q: While traveling in the Valley recently, I found my trip hampered not once but twice by slow-moving tractors in the roadway. After both encounters ended in horn blasts and a few choice words, I began to wonder, just exactly how long is long enough to wait behind this sort of slow-moving rural roadblock before a person is allowed to react in the manner in which I did? NAME WITHHELD

A: The Rio Grande Valley, with its rich, loamy soils and subtropical climate, is the fruit basket of the state. And the vegetable basket, the cotton basket, the sorghum basket, and the sugarcane basket. And anytime you drive through a basket, you're bound to have some trouble. You see, even though some of the basket's produce does grow on actual trees, none of it grows on metaphorical ones. These crops are carefully cultivated by farmers who work sunup to sundown so that you will have food to, as President George W. Bush once said, put on your family. And farmers don't go places in a hurry. In fact, the way the Texanist sees it, the farmer's role in society is not only to grow our foods and fibers but also to maintain our connection to the slow pace of nature. It is not unusual to experience a miles-long, teeth-grinding, fist-shaking tantrum when stuck behind one of these salts of the earth, perched up on his tractor like a pasha on an elephant, but it is not an admirable response. Next time you get caught tailing a tractor that's chugging along a good forty or fifty miles per hour below the posted speed limit, try to enjoy the bucolic fields and orchards. And give a wave of thanks to those who work them. You wouldn't bite the hand that feeds, so why should you bark obscenities at it? Not only do farmers provide the food that ends up on your table (or family), but they can also give you a much-needed excuse to slow down. ★

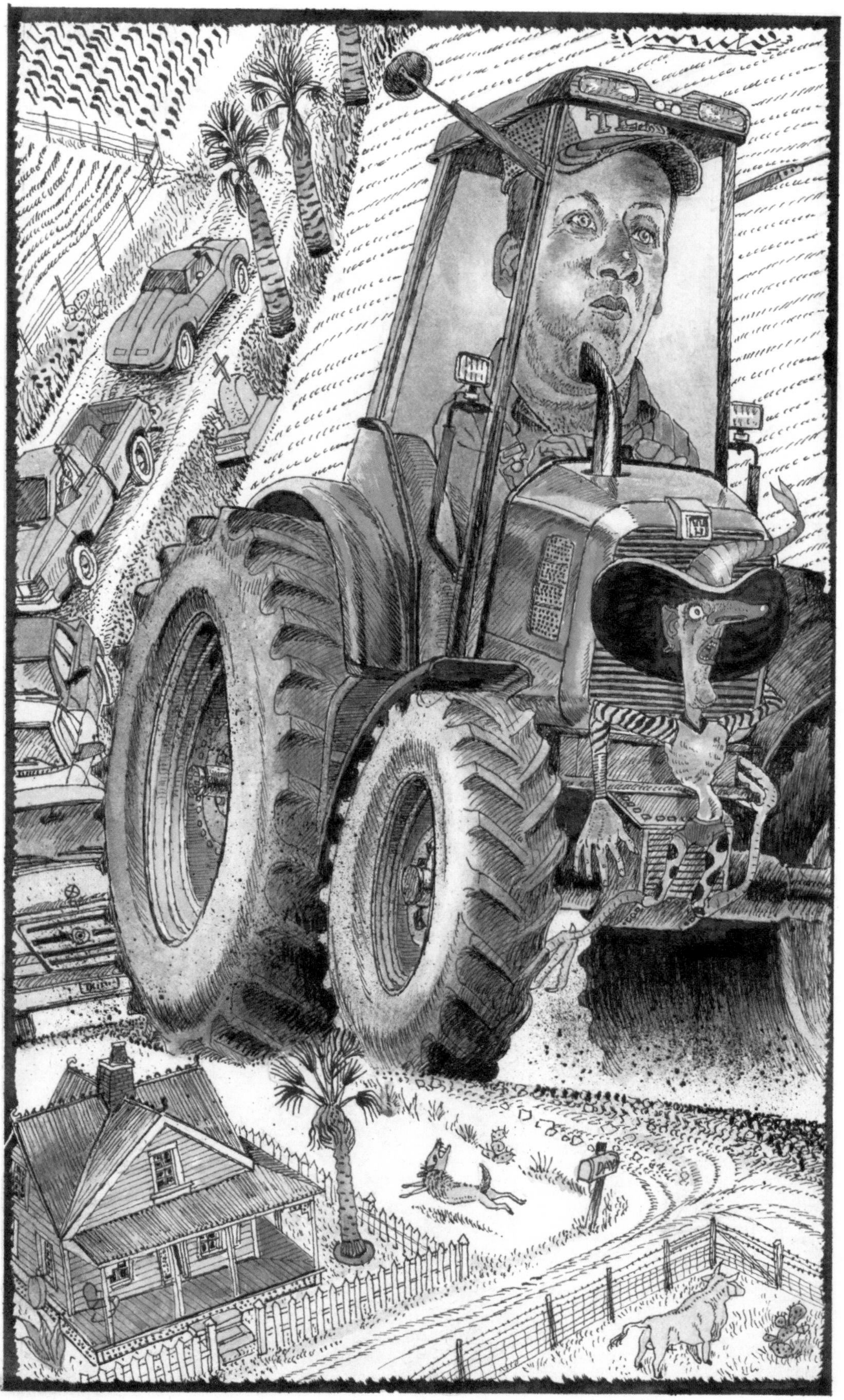

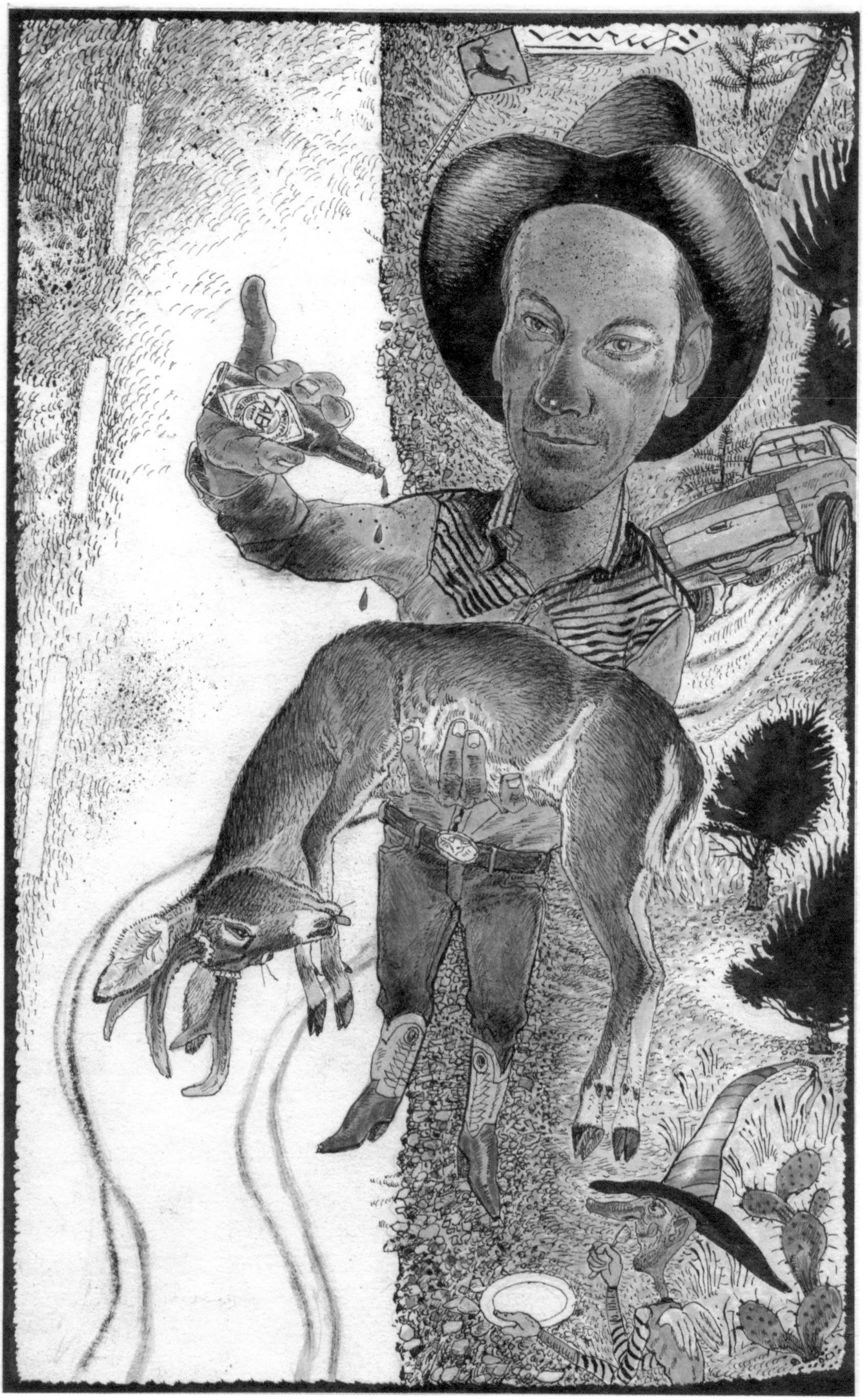

Q: I live near Wimberley, and recently, as I was driving home from a PTA meeting, I hit and killed a deer. My question is, if I had acted fast, could I have legally eaten that deer? And if I could have, should I have? And if I should have, how would you recommend preparing road-killed deer?
BILL EARLY, WIMBERLEY

A: You don't need to log many miles on Texas roads to conclude that the white-tailed deer is a superabundant, reckless, even suicidal creature. The Texanist can barely drive to the grocery store without spotting one prancing along the shoulder, threatening at any minute to commence a mismatched game of chicken with his '95 Chevy. Our byways are littered with the bloated carcasses of the cloven-hoofed losers of these contests. But while it is commonly assumed that to all victors belong all spoils, this is a rare instance in which they do not. It may seem wasteful, but it would have been illegal, according to Texas state law, for you to have field-dressed the kill, thrown it into the back of your truck, and headed home to light the grill.

The Texanist himself is a lover of venison. But imagine for a moment what might happen if the practice of roadkill collection and consumption was legal and accepted behavior: Plenty of ol' boys would seize the chance to turn their F-150s into weapons. The thought of them out cruising the highways for dinner, swerving this way and that, plowing through fences and over bar ditches in frenzied pursuit of their prey is terrifying to contemplate. How long before some kid's dog gets run down? And then what? Could they eat the dog? The Texanist can tell you that within a month's time our thoroughfares would be baited with corn and completely unsafe for the average motorist. Roadkill, tasty though it may appear, is best left on the road. ★

Q: I grew up on a gravel road and was always taught that it was good manners to drive slowly enough to avoid raising dust when around people's houses. But folks today seem to just speed by going 90 miles per hour, not caring where the dust settles. Is there such a thing as gravel-road etiquette, and if so, how best can I teach it to the neighbors? PEGGY MULLARD, MCLENNAN COUNTY

A: There is indeed such a thing as gravel-road etiquette, and congratulations to you for being familiar with it. The Texanist received such instruction before he was even of legal driving age (this was on the back routes of Bell County, where the Texanist's father assumed that the impact on people and property would be limited). The rules are simple: Don't stir up too much dust around homes (or anywhere else for that matter); when running over rattlers, stomp on the brakes hard enough to rip them to shreds; and acknowledge oncoming vehicles (and anybody else for that matter) with a friendly wave. City folk, with whom the state of Texas seems more and more congested, may require some help grasping these particulars. Think of a waterway's no-wake zones, which are intended to keep boat captains from creating bothersome chop that can lap too vigorously upon things that shouldn't be lapped upon. A rural road's no-dust zones are much the same, but swap the boat's wake for a thick cloud of dust, which will blanket the surrounding area—cars, children, and pets included. The problem is that no-wake zones are designated by way of well-marked and easily visible buoys, while no-dust zones are demarcated by nothing more than common courtesy shared between good country folk. Maybe it's time for the introduction of a few dry-land buoys, which when anchored along a roadside are sometimes called signs, to get your message across. Ruralites tend to be an industrious sort, and this should be an easy project for you. Here are a few ideas to help get your creative juices flowing: "Raise Children, Not Dust," "Go Slow or Go to Hell," "If I Eat Dust, You'll Eat Lead," "Raise Dust, Bite Dust," and "Slow the Hell Down." One or all of these displayed on the road near your house should have some effect. Keep the Texanist posted. ★

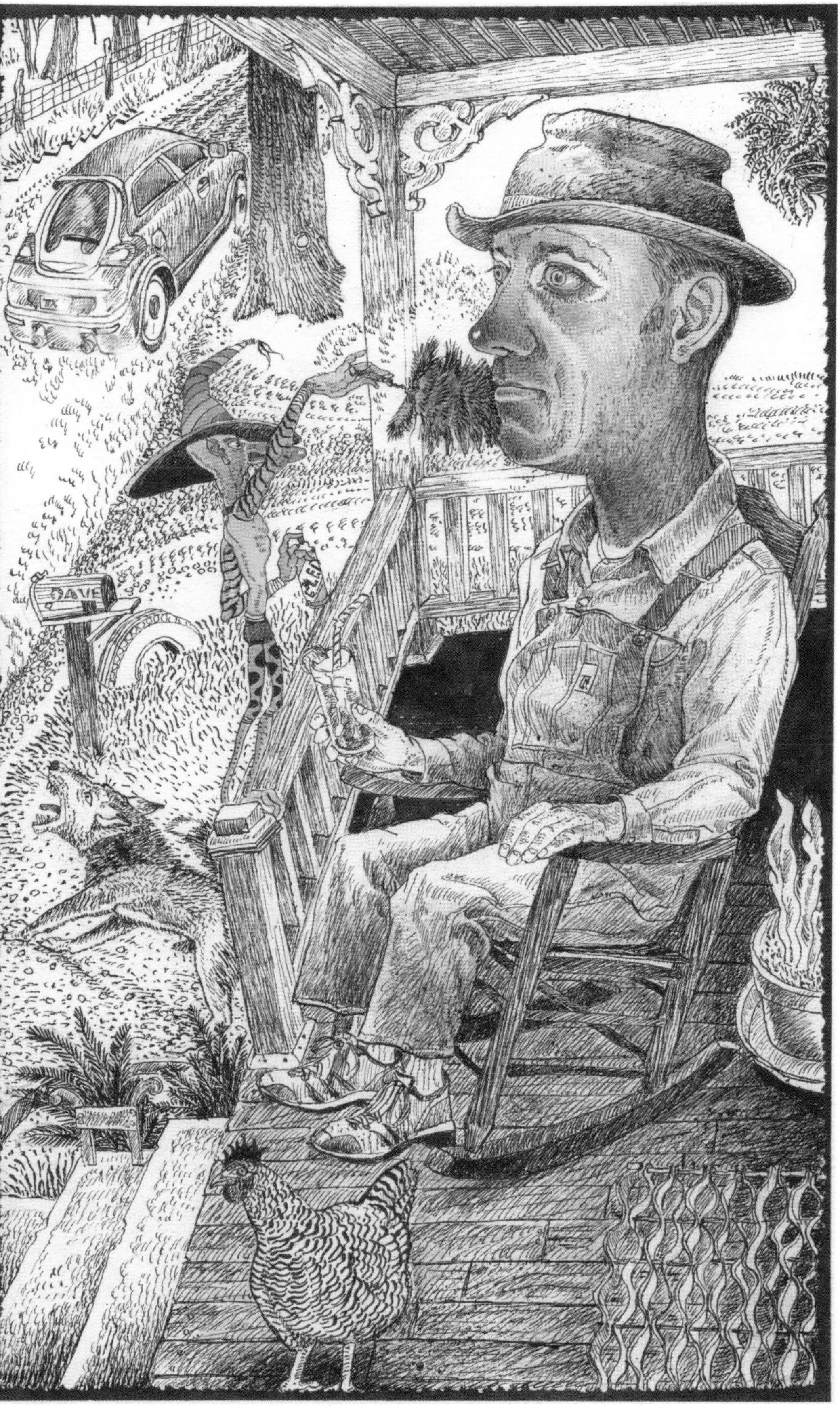
TX
DAVE

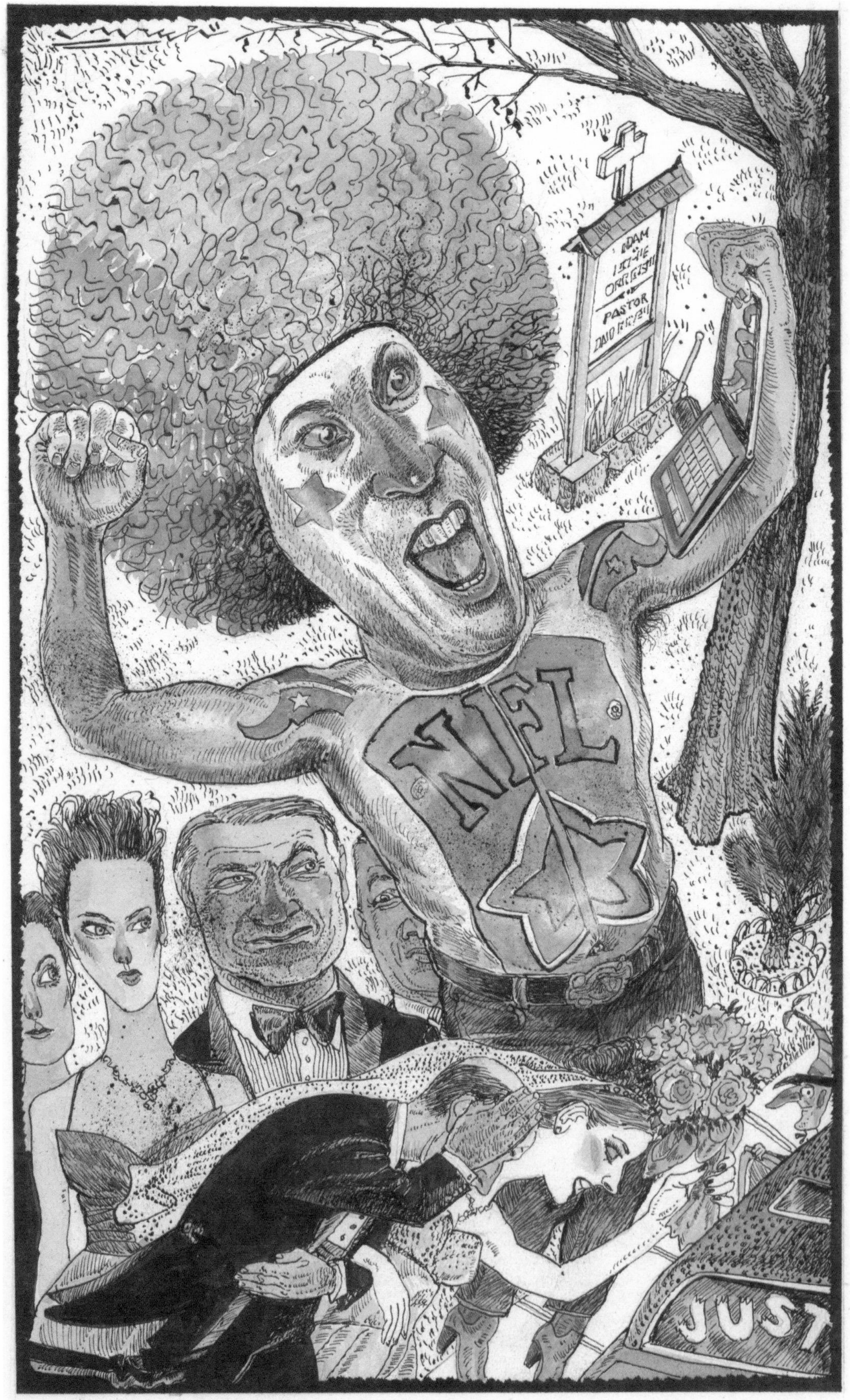
PASTOR
NFL
JUST

Q: My wife has just informed me that we will be attending her college roommate's wedding, which is to be held in Phoenix on the first Sunday in February. The problem, as you are likely aware, is that this is Super Bowl Sunday. Who plans a wedding on Super Bowl Sunday? Secondly, how do I get out of going? NAME WITHHELD, DALLAS

A: The Texanist dimly recalls having once been involved in a covert operation at the postnuptial festivities of a forgotten (to him, at least) friend of his missus, during which he and a dozen or so other spouses, fiancés, boyfriends, uncles, nephews, cousins, a waiter, a cellist, and a ring bearer skipped the dancing, toasts, and cake and piled into the back of the idling wedding limo to watch the final innings of game six of the 1993 World Series on the twelve-inch TV. Despite the threat of discovery and public scorn, this particular mission had a successful outcome (especially for the cellist, a Blue Jays fan). But in truth, it is never much fun to watch a game while constantly looking over your shoulder for the hand that will grab your ear and drag you, feebly protesting, back to the buffet. The Texanist should know. In search of (the) game, he has also slipped away from—and been firmly returned to—funerals, baptisms, one bris, a couple of quinceañeras, and children's birthday parties too numerous and cake-smeared to recall. But that was all before the invention of a small, miraculous device known as the smartphone. As you and the Texanist both know, without first getting out of your own marriage, there is no way you are getting out of going to Phoenix for the most ill-timed wedding since the Von Whosits tied the knot on the upper deck of the Hindenburg. But unlike the Texanist back in 1993, you have options. Instead of stealing away to the dressing room, lobby bar, upstairs bedroom, or hotel kitchen, nowadays any interested party can simply sneak a peek at his phone. Just make sure the shindig is not in some remote Sonoran Desert locale unlikely to have reception or Wi-Fi. In case that it is, the Texanist recommends trying the limo. ★

Q: Recently, my sister's family visited for a weekend. My 7-year-old niece, who is constantly out of control and never disciplined, was flying around like a banshee, and she crashed into a bureau and knocked over four bottles of Dublin Dr Pepper that my husband bought on eBay. They all smashed on the tile floor. My sister didn't do anything, so I disciplined my niece myself. She started crying, and they left in a huff. My sister says I overreacted. I say she underreacted. What do you say? NAME WITHHELD

A: The Texanist is sorry for your loss and would begin with a simple observation. He finds it telling that after many long years of your niece's unregulated misbehavior, the act that finally caused you to ferociously erupt in righteous anger like a roaring volcano of justice was not the tracking of mud across a Persian carpet or the thwacking of buds off an heirloom rosebush but the wanton destruction of four eternally nonreturnable eight-ounce bottles of Imperial Sugar–sweetened Texas history. You are, very clearly, a person after the Texanist's own heart. And so was your response to this unfortunate incident in keeping with what the Texanist's would have been, more or less. Parents should be able to control their children, plain and simple. Your niece should not have been tearing through the house like a wrecking ball, and her mother should not have let it all go down without applying a dose of parental correction. Were this the first time such a scene had been witnessed, the Texanist might advise restraint, but when a problem is chronic, as this seems to be, there is no better remedy than the smart snap of a good tongue-lashing. Some of what you rained down has probably soaked in by now, with the rest running off and flowing beneath the proverbial bridge, so the Texanist suggests that you follow up with your sis. Give her a call, and don't let her off the hook until the disagreement is sorted out. Like it or not, blood is thicker than even discontinued Dublin Dr Pepper, delicious though it may be. ★

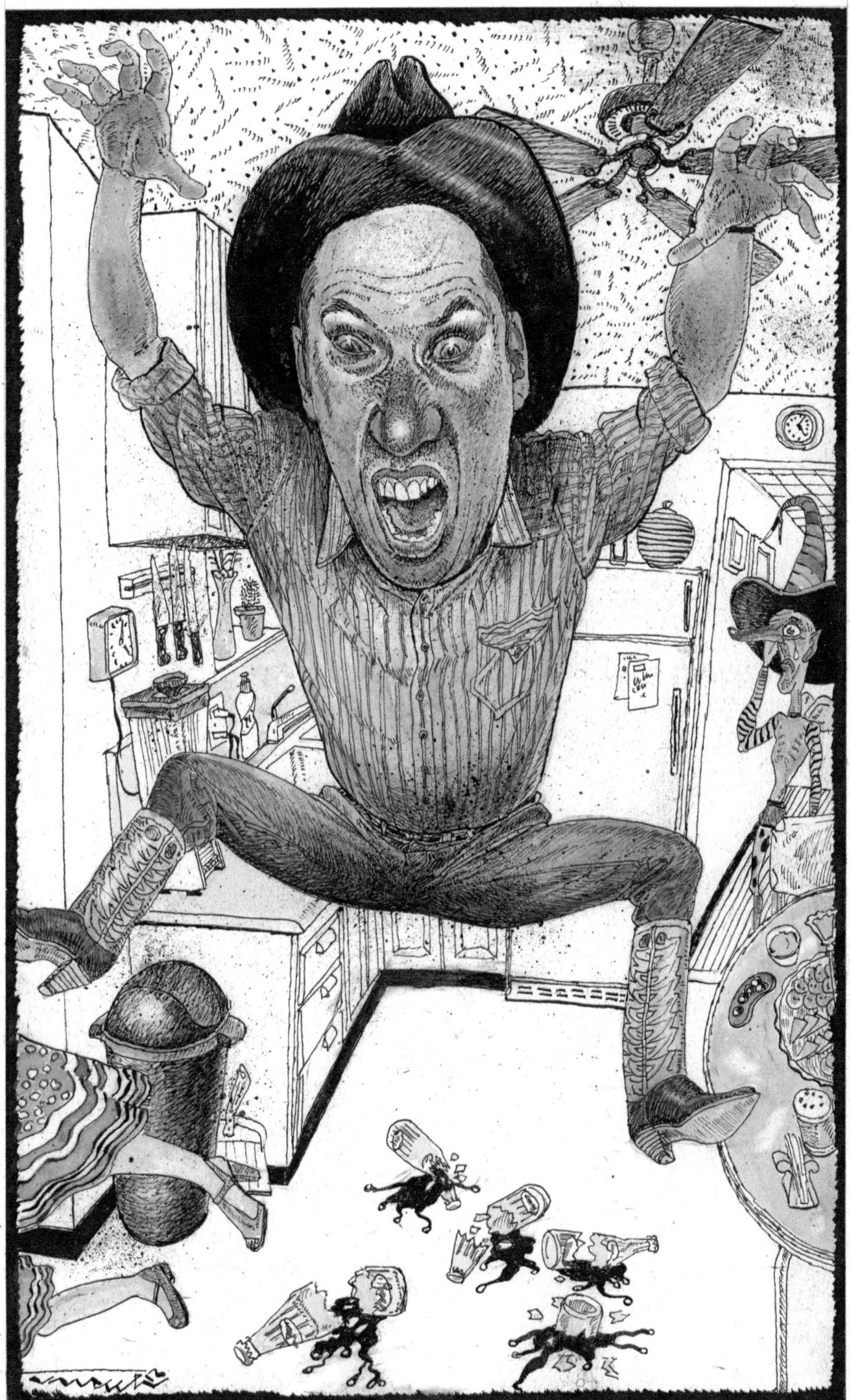

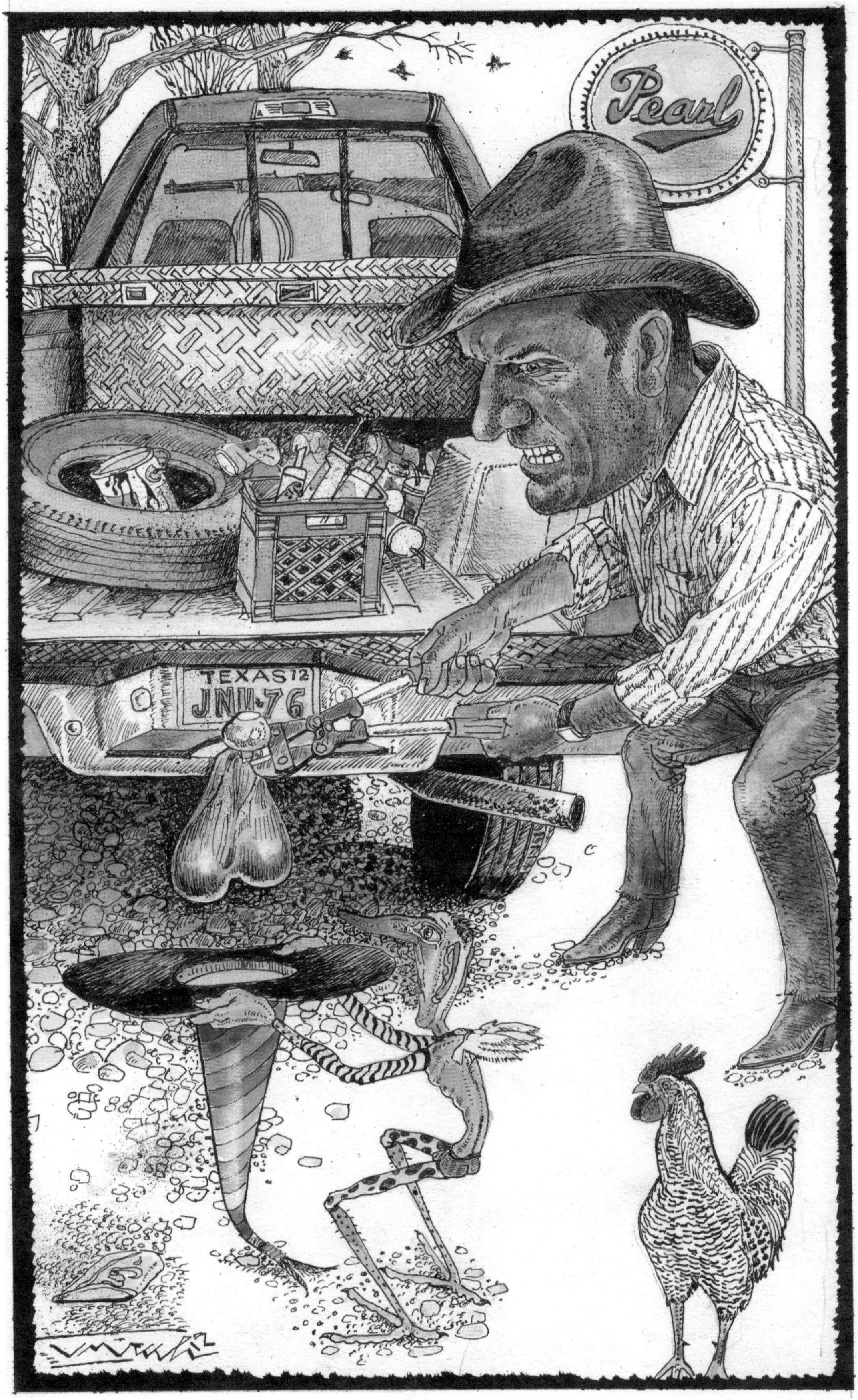
Pearl
TEXAS 12
JNU-76

Q: Lately I have seen a growing number of vehicles with ornamental testicles hanging from the rear bumper. At first I thought they were supposed to be bull testicles, but now they are showing up in all different colors and at least two different shapes. I think this is absolutely ridiculous, but I have been accused of being no fun. I really need the Texanist's opinion on this particular matter. Is this okay?   CASEY BRADSHAW, MABANK

A: The only acceptable balls to have attached to the back of your car or truck are chrome hitch ones. They are used for towing things. So you are advised to immediately lodge a counteraccusation of barbarism against whomever it is that has accused you of being no fun, for by doing so that person has established an appalling fact: that he or she is tickled by ornamental testicles. This person should cower in shame. The Texanist has glimpsed these unfortunate bumper accoutrements out on the road, and he is here to tell you that you are absolutely correct. Adorning the rear end of a truck or SUV with a rubber pair can be considered nothing but ridiculous. Actually, it can be considered a few more things: ugly, unseemly, uncouth, and hopelessly redneck. In fact, the Texanist knows plenty of rednecks for whom these dangling decorative gonads are even too redneck. And what is the point of these vehicular show balls anyway? Are they supposed to somehow impress and intimidate other automobiles, like an unneutered pit bull at the dog park? This is a rare case in which the Texanist has no earthly idea why people do what they do. If you are a person who has ever attached a pair of costume car cojones to your rear bumper, please write to the Texanist and explain this cretinous practice. If indeed you know how to write. ★

Q: I've attended weekend dances going way back to the sixties, when I was a little girl, and I just recently realized that the folks on the dance floor always scoot in a counterclockwise fashion. Do country dancers ever go clockwise? COURTNEY CHISUM, FORT WORTH

A: Congratulations to you on your keen powers of observation. Indeed, it is accepted boot-scooting canon that, be it the two-step, waltz, cotton-eyed Joe, or schottische, the standard direction in which the light fantastic is tripped in a Texas dance hall is counterclockwise. Theories as to why the line of dance, as it is known in dancing circles, moves in this way range from ridiculous bunkum having to do with the Coriolis effect or short-left-leggedness to tales of Old World hoedowns where right-handed men needed to be ever ready to draw a sword from a scabbard on the left hip. The truth will likely never be known. Are there circumstances in which dancers turn a blind eye to the long-held custom and go clockwise around the hardwood? Sure, it's not unheard of. Sometimes, toward the end of a particularly festive evening, after a good many longnecks have been drained, a dancer may become momentarily turned around and unknowingly begin crashing his terrified partner headlong through the oncoming stream. The Texanist has witnessed this firsthand, and it is not a pretty sight. Depending on the size of the misguided dancer and the tempo of the song, it can result in serious injury. In fact, he dimly recalls having been involved in such a pileup himself, but the incomplete, flickering images he retains from that tragic evening (flying boots, trampled hats, screaming ladies) are too disturbing to pursue. Best to just go with the flow. ★

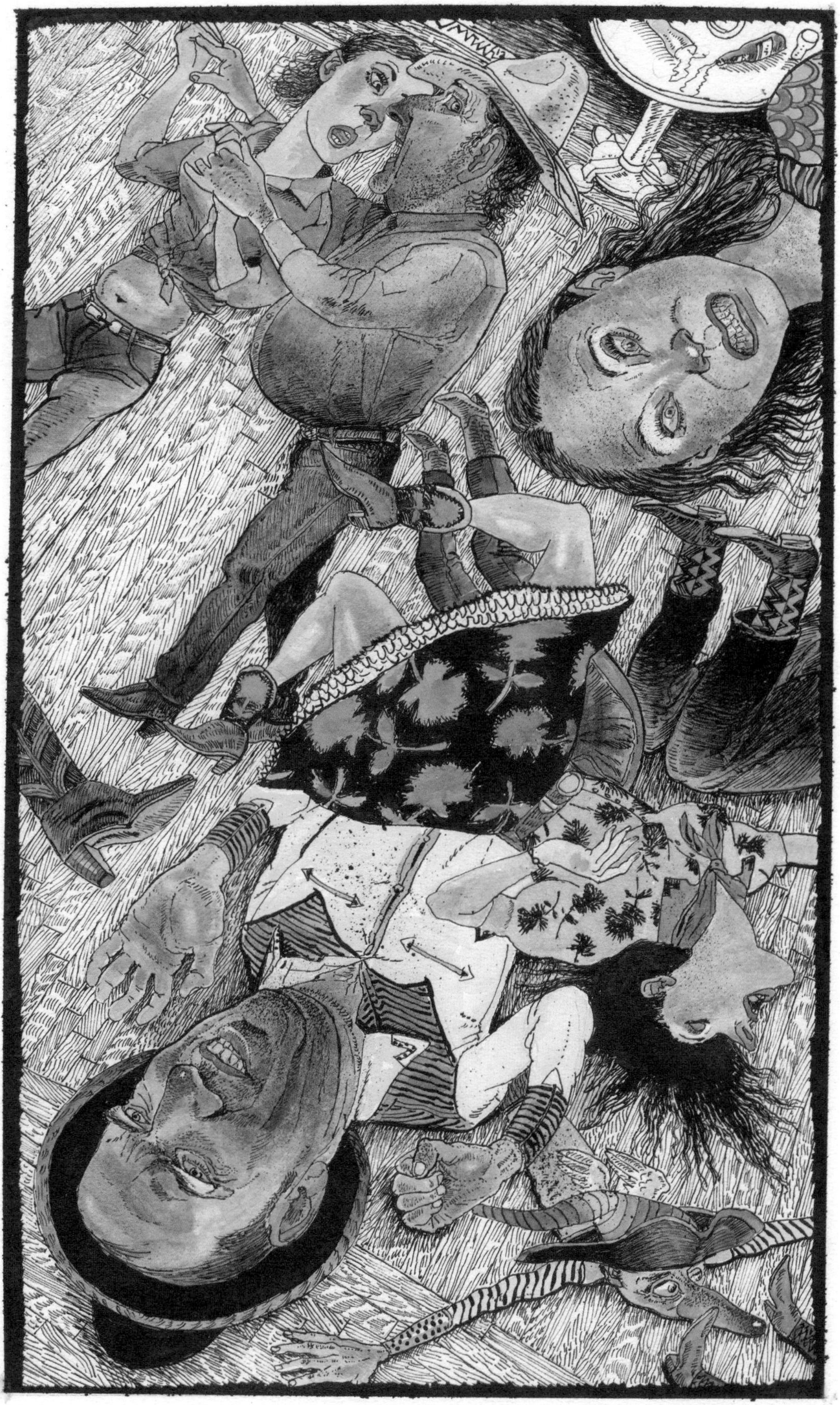

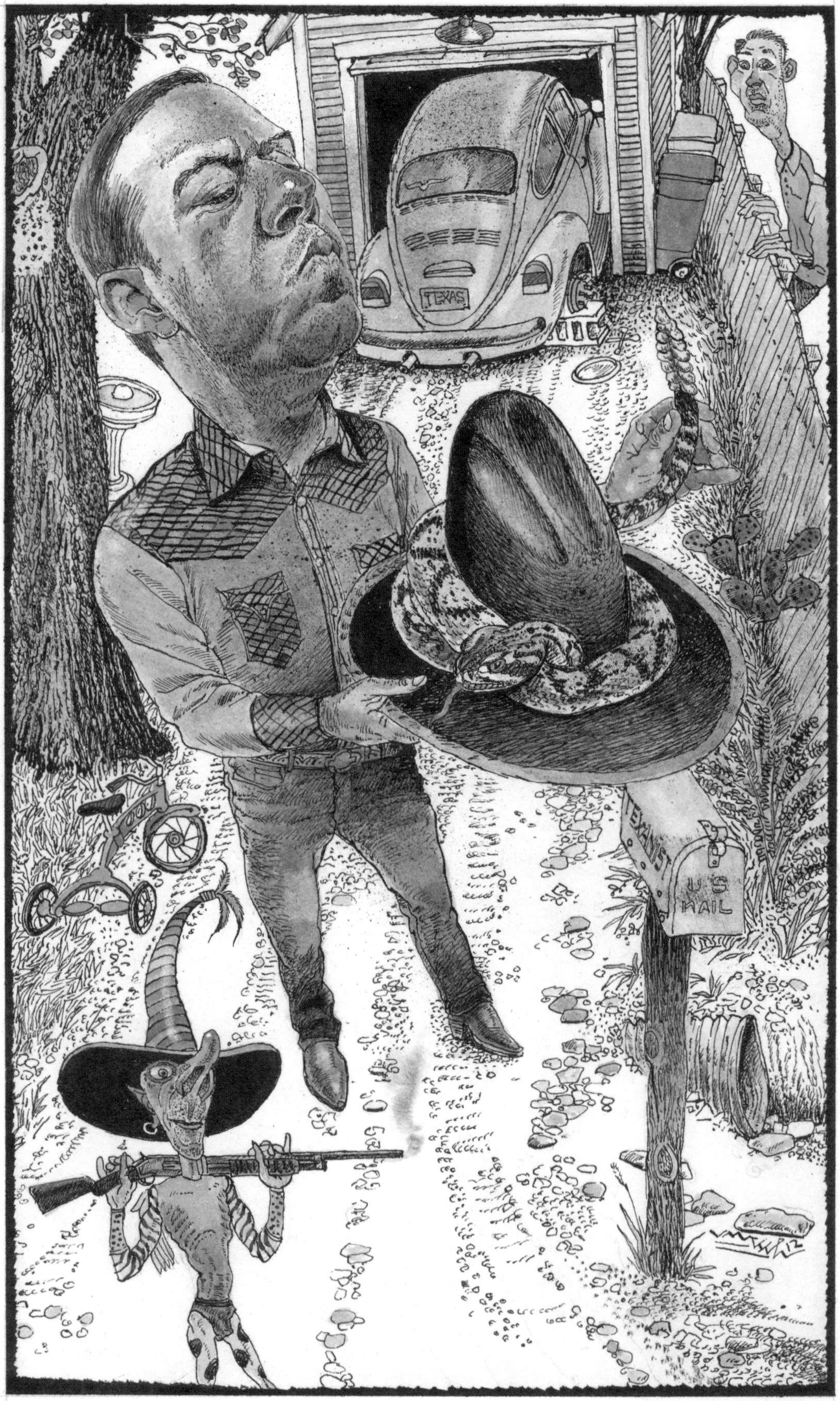
TEXAS
U S
MAIL

Q: I live in a subdivision on the western edge of San Antonio, and recently I found a fairly large rattlesnake in my backyard. I reacted just as I was taught by my daddy to react in such a situation: with one blast from a 20-gauge. This alarmed my neighbors, and now I feel like they look down on me as some sort of rowdy hillbilly, which I can assure you I am not. I don't see how I could have handled the encounter any differently. Do you?

NAME WITHHELD

A: There was a time, about a century ago, when almost the entirety of the state's citizenry made their homes outside our bustling urban centers. These were sturdy, self-reliant, God- (and snake-) fearing people. People like your father, who took care of many a perceived threat with a barrel or two of hot lead. But according to the last census figures, the state's population of hearty country folk has dwindled to a paltry 15.3 percent. As ruralists pull up stakes and move to town with the newly arrived Californians, our metropolitan areas respond by expanding into the hitherto-rural hinterlands. What was Old Brown's back four hundred yesterday is the brand-new Colinas de Serpientes de Cascabel subdivision today. But in the midst of our transition to a state full of urbanites and suburbanites, some Texans (the Texanist is looking at you) have managed to hold on to their rural roots just as firmly as they have clung to their scatterguns. The old saying, it seems, sometimes holds true: You can take the shotgun-toting boy out of the country, but you just can't take the shotgun out of the country boy's hands. The thing is, while a thunderous discharge—whether it be focused in the general direction of a dove, sporting clay, old rusty bucket, or supposed venomous trespasser—may be nothing to you, your less-countrified neighbors are sure to frown, as they have, on such a ruckus. So will your local law enforcers. Like it or not, the new realities of your changing environs would have you leave the gun under the bed and the snake to the professionals, who will "take care of it"—albeit in a slightly different manner than that of your daddy. ⋆

Q: Recently, I had a dog show up on my property and make itself at home. He didn't have a collar or anything to identify him, but I suspected that he belonged to a man down the road who keeps a bunch of dogs for hog hunting. The thing is, I got pretty attached and now I don't want to give him back. And I bet he doesn't want me to either. Hog hunting is dangerous work. Have I done the wrong thing? NAME WITHHELD

A: The Texanist is familiar with both sides of this conundrum. On the one hand, there have been many long, dark nights of the soul in which his spirits have been buoyed by the doggy affections of a loyal and puffy bichon frise named Lulu (the Texanist's missus assures him that a man's manliness has nothing whatsoever to do with the size of his dog). Yet he has also dispatched more than one feral pig while it was being firmly subdued by a snarling team of rough and large South Texas hog dogs. Which is to say, he knows well the cozy camaraderie of a pampered pooch but is not blind to the fact that canines were put on earth to aid man in more than simply fetching his slippers. The dilemma in which you have ensnarled yourself is a real doozy, but the facts are the facts, and your own guilty conscience is telling you the same thing that the Texanist will repeat for you now: The dog—noble, brown-eyed, tail-wagging, slobbery, kiss-giving beast that he is—does not belong to you. And you know it. But depending on just how reasonable a man your hog-slaughtering neighbor is, all hope may or may not be lost. The Texanist advises you to make your way down the road (after first alerting an emergency contact to your destination and when to expect you back), explain the situation, and attempt to strike a deal. You may end up paying with cold, hard cash; time spent cleaning his kennels; an understanding handshake; or a years-long feud, but if you really want to legitimize your relationship with the dog, it's vital that you at least make an attempt to reconcile. Other than having ol' Spot ripped from your hands with a yelp or the most vicious of his former colleagues sicced on you, what's the worst that could happen? ⋆

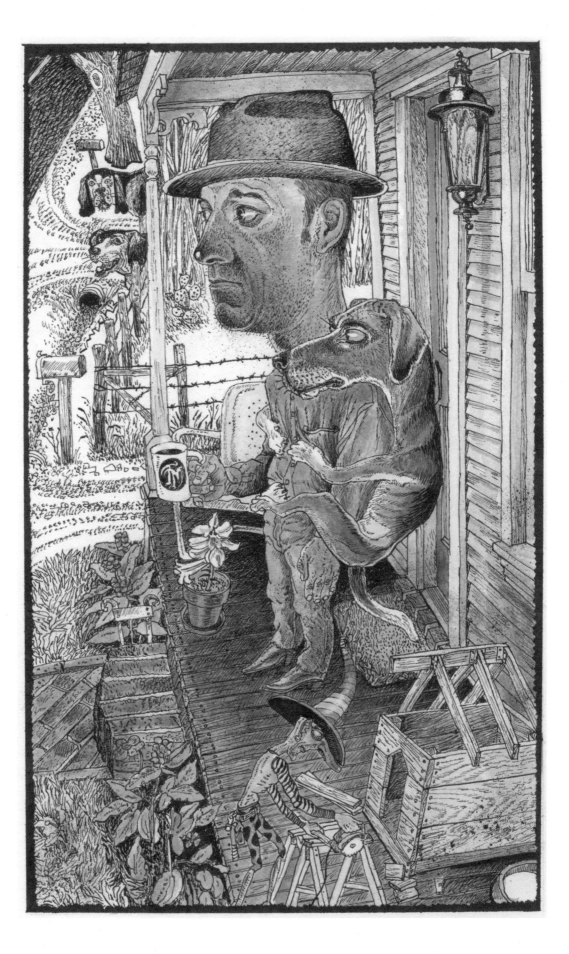

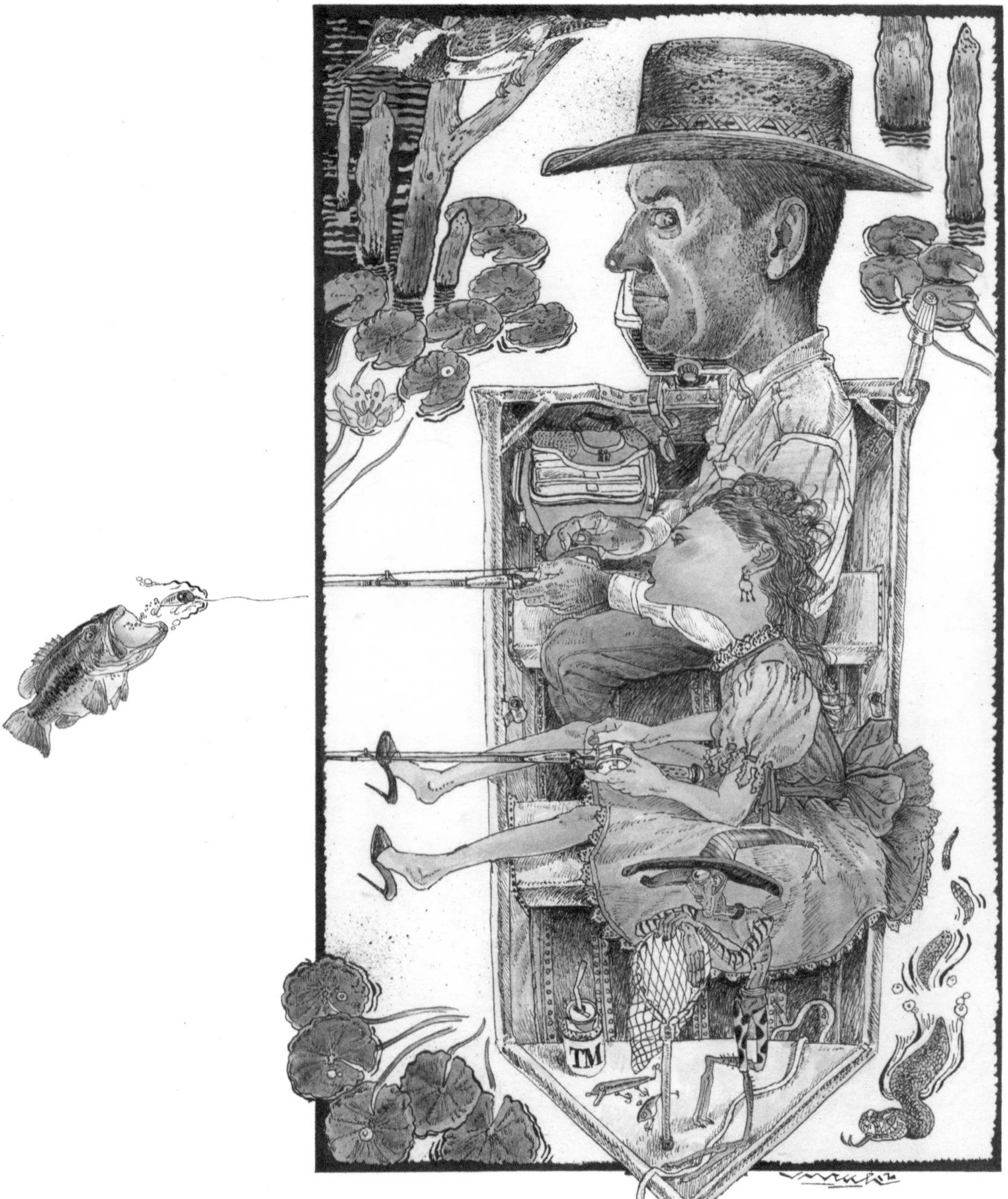
TM

Q: My 12-year-old daughter is a complete and unashamed tomboy. She hunts with me, fishes with me, and throws the football with me. Wouldn't be caught dead in a dress. I love every second of it, but her mother thinks it's come time for her to drop some of these boyish pursuits and start acting and dressing more like a "lady." I hate to lose my little pardner, but is the girl's mom right? Could all these manly endeavors leave a permanent mark as she develops into womanhood? NAME WITHHELD

A: The Texanist comes from a long line of hardy Texas women. He also married a hardy Texas woman and, in time, begot a small Texas woman just as hardy as the one you have described. Football? *Check*. Fishing? *Check*. Dirty fingernails, perpetually scabby knees, good horsemanship? *Check*. Handy with a bow and arrow, unflappable in the face of weird bugs, vehemently opposed to skirts? *Checks all around*. Needless to say, this sweet little hellion is the apple (sometimes the crab apple) of the Texanist's eye and a shining example of the trademark sturdiness for which Texas women are known all over the world. Where does it come from? As determined by a pseudoscientific study commissioned long ago by the Texanist, there is simply something in the water (subsequent attempts, however, to bottle and sell this clear elixir across state lines were unsuccessful). Not only is your daughter's tomboyishness nothing for you or her mother to fret over, it is her birthright. That joie de vivre, effervescence, bumptiousness, and even, please pardon the Texanist, ballsiness that you've come to love in her are merely the traits of a full-grown Texas woman in the making. Besides, the peer pressure, social mores, and discovery of boys that come with adolescence will soon serve to smooth out the rougher edges. This is when the Texanist would advise you to commence the real worrying. ★

Q: I've had a tailgate party in the same spot for just about every Aggie home game since R. C. Slocum's last season, in 2002. This year I'd like to make the move to a different spot, on the other side of the stadium, but it's between two established tailgates and I don't know the folks who host them. Are there any guidelines for busting in and setting up a new tailgate?
HOWARD MARPLES, HOUSTON

A: That all depends on what sort of tailgate you are planning to bust in and set up. Is it one of those gigantic, bottomless-keg bashes that boast a mouthwatering spread of professionally catered grub, multiple sixty-inch plasma televisions, and a prescheduled appearance by your alma mater's marching band's percussion section? As anyone who has ever attended a football game—be it professional, collegiate, powder-puff, or peewee—in the great state of Texas well knows, there is a spectrum of tailgate ostentation along which these festive pregame shindigs may be plotted. At one end is the aforementioned five-star jamboree, complete with its own power grid and kitchen staff; at the other, it's just two guys sharing pigskin pleasantries and a flask of contraband bourbon while enjoying a bag of cold McNuggets. Though the bigger parties tend to provide the neighbors with more perks ("Hey, y'all, this commercial-sized chafing dish full of pork tamales ain't gonna eat itself!"), their size and spectacle can be intrusive. There is a common bond that binds any home game's tailgaters, but that bond can be strained by the roar of a dozen generators kicking on at once. Nonetheless, even a comically ginormous party can be wedged in if the approach is tactful. Which is to say, keep those tamales coming, and be sure to give your neighbors ample warning before the bass drums arrive. Also keep in mind that tailgate real estate is often held in perpetuity by way of the honor system, so make sure you're not violating the sacrosanctity of that code. And you should further verify that the spot is in an open-access site and there are no official hoops (fees, permits, etc.) to jump through. If the answers to those questions are "I'm not" and "There ain't," then the Texanist wouldn't hesitate, not for one tick of the clock, to pull up stakes and put them down anew on the other side of Kyle Field. Just let a thumbs-up and a hearty "Gig 'em!" be your introduction. ★

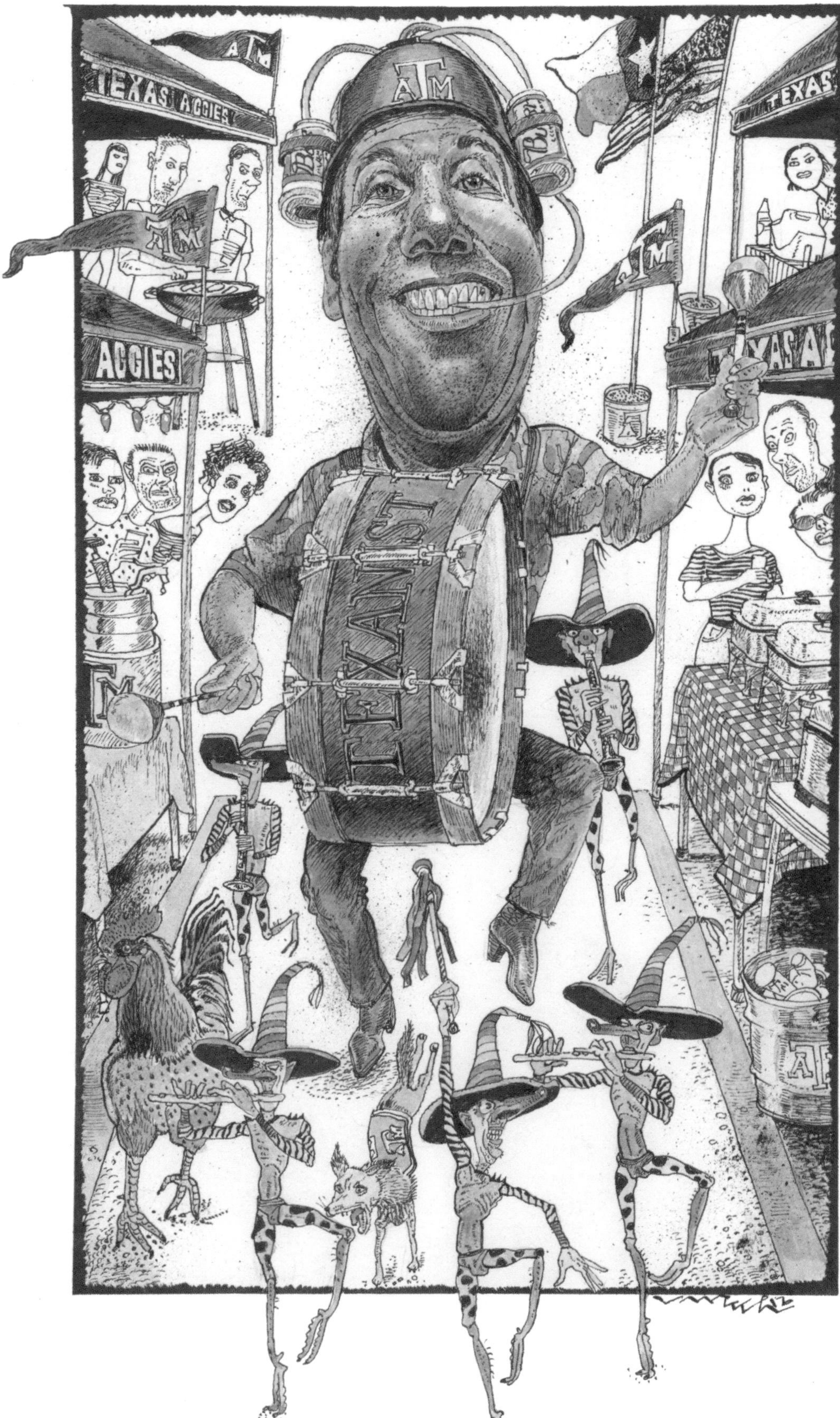
TEXAS AGGIES
AGGIES
TEXAS

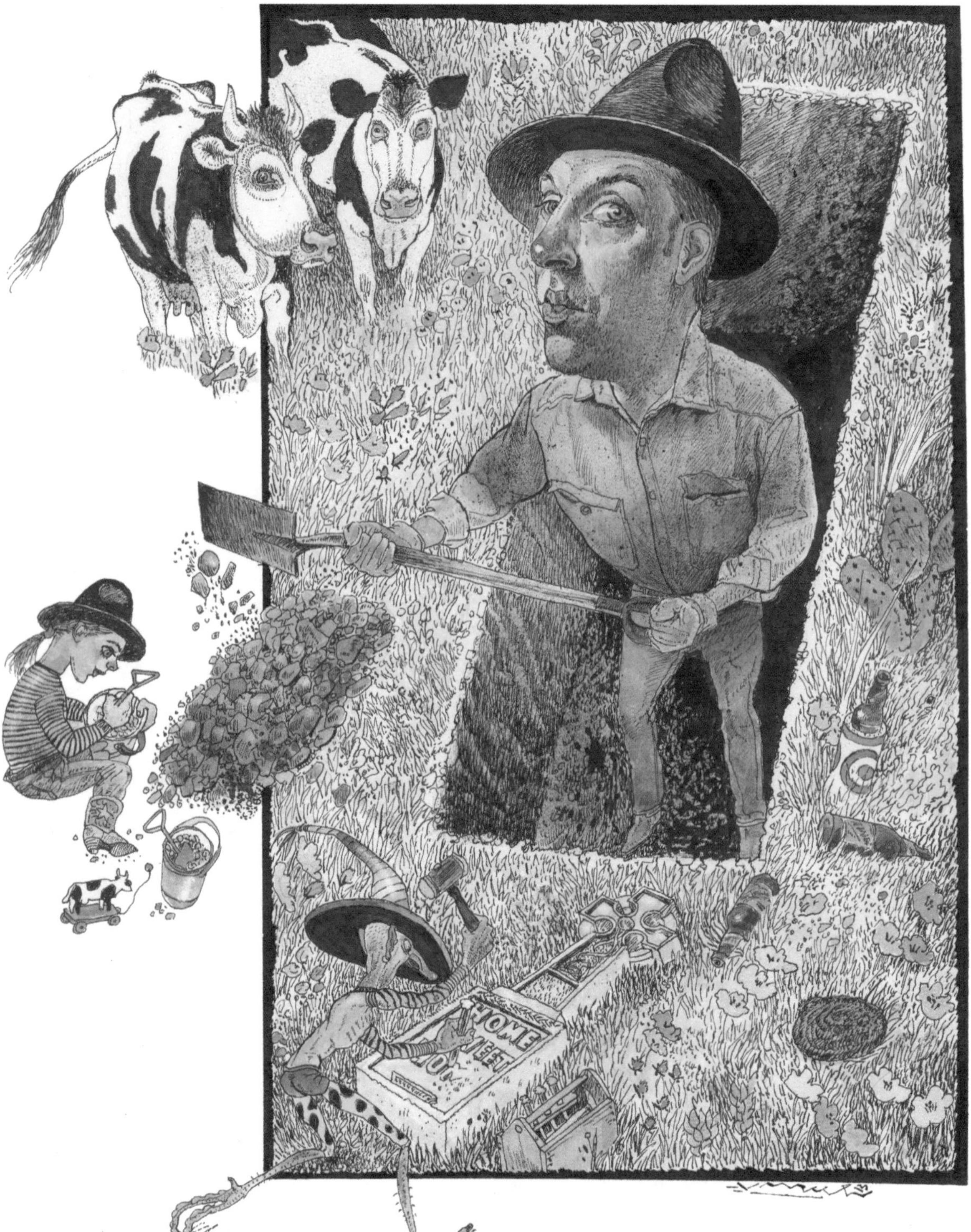
HOME

Q: My wife and I are working toward finally buying some property in Washington County to retire on and have a place for the kids and grandkids to come and enjoy the simple life on occasion. I would like to know if it is legal, when the time comes to pass on to that great pasture in the sky, for us to be buried on our own property. Do we need a special license?

M. CERMAK, ACKERLY

A: The Texanist hopes that it is a good long while before you and your missus have the opportunity to push up the trademark Washington County bluebonnets. But he is very much in favor of y'all's doing so, when the time does come, from the comfort of your own family boneyard. Why bother with the clamor and din of a public cemetery when you can opt for the peaceful convenience of at-home eternal rest right there in the family patch? Cermak Cemetery has a nice ring to it. There are, however, some red-tape-adorned hoops to jump through before you can actually break ground, and since no one's getting any younger, you are wise to get the ball rolling. The Texas Funeral Service Commission, the agency responsible for the ultimate disposition of most dead Texans, recommends that before burying yourself you check with the county authorities to ensure that you don't run afoul of any local rules or regulations dealing with deed restrictions, flood plains, underground pipelines or cabling, and the like. The good folks at the Funeral Service Commission and your county clerk's office will provide the rest of the details and help guide you along your journey. Once all your ducks (and plots) are in a row, it'll be time to think about the finer details: creaky gates, rusty fencing, and some tall grass for the wind to spookily rustle 'neath the full moon. Do you have the number of a good grave digger? Have you thought of an epitaph? Maybe something like "Here Lies M. Cermak, Husband, Father, Grandfather, Cemetery Establisher." That's okay, but it's a little clunky. Needs some work. Luckily, you've still got time for that. ★

Q: A sizable possum has started making nightly trips across my back porch, and it's driving my two dogs nuts. I don't like possums at all, so I've been thinking about just sliding the door open one of these nights and letting the dogs go after it. Is this one of those things that I will regret afterward?
SAMANTHA VERA, HOUSTON

A: This letter hits unusually close to home for the Texanist. One recent night, he opened the back door to let his family dog, Lulu, out for the last of her patrols. A loyal and puffy bichon frise, Lulu currently possesses only three of her original four legs, yet she is still a fast dog when she means to be, and before the Texanist could react, she darted toward the garage, which is separate from the house. The Texanist's keen eyes quickly detected the source of her excitement: a midsize, scrabbling varmint heading for the garage's open door. Not wanting the filthy creature to seek refuge among his pristine gardening implements and boxes of old taxes, the Texanist sprang into action, dashing across the yard with such speed that his bathrobe flew up behind him, revealing to the neighbors nearly all of his pale and impressive physique. Unfortunately, just as he leaped through the open door and attempted to slam it shut from the inside to keep the creature out, the thing tried to back itself through the door to escape Lulu's ferocious and incessant yapping. The Texanist, barefoot and partially exposed, wound up with a large, writhing possum pinned to the doorjamb, its hind end inside and its hissing and tooth-filled head outside. Holding the door–cum–snap trap tightly, the Texanist considered his options. He could stand against the door until daylight, with the possum secured, hoping that Lulu would remain at a safe distance on the other side. Or he could open the door and risk the silvery beast's attacking Lulu (or the Texanist's own unshod feet) or disappearing ominously into some dark corner of the garage to die a smelly death. None of these options were appealing. Nor was there any sort of weapon within reach. Fortunately, the hullabaloo had rousted Mrs. Texanist, a hardy sort, who emerged on the back porch for the following exchange:

> Mrs. Texanist: What the %*$@#& are y'all doing out there?
> Texanist: Grab Lulu! Run down here and grab Lulu!
> Mrs. Texanist: Where are you?
> Texanist: Inside the damn garage. Hurry up! I've got a possum in the door! I can't open it!
> Mrs. Texanist: Why'd you do that?
> Texanist: Can't get into it right now, babe! Just get Lulu!

Sound of boots clomping across the yard, followed by renewed hissing from the possum, a whimper from Lulu, boots clomping back across the yard, and the door to the house slamming shut.

Texanist: Thanks, hon.

After that, the situation resolved itself quickly. The Texanist grabbed a broom, shooed the possum out the door, fastened the door, refastened his sash, and returned to the house. The point of this story is that the Texanist, like everybody, has ample reason to dislike possums, and yet even he cannot bring himself to condone the violence that would ensue if you released your hounds into the backyard to tear the critter limb from limb. That is simply not sporting. Just keep the dogs in the house. And make sure the garage door is securely closed. ★

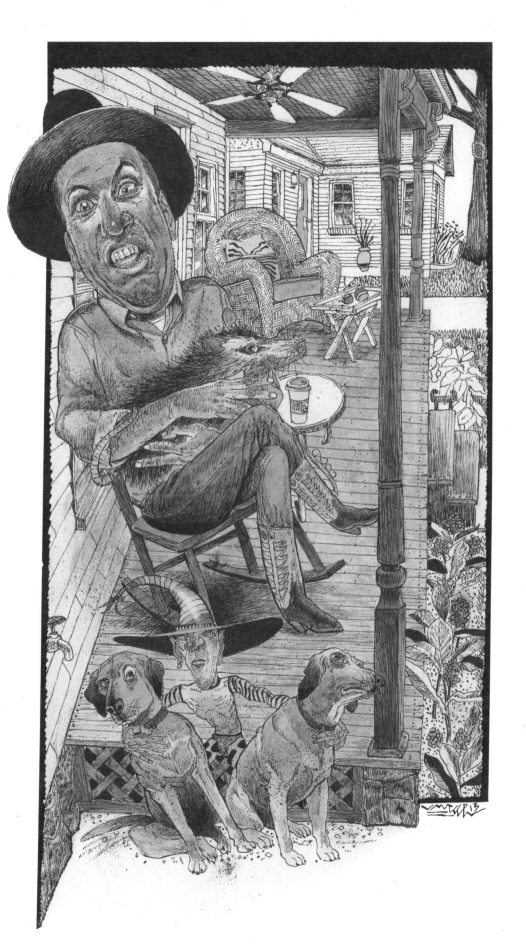

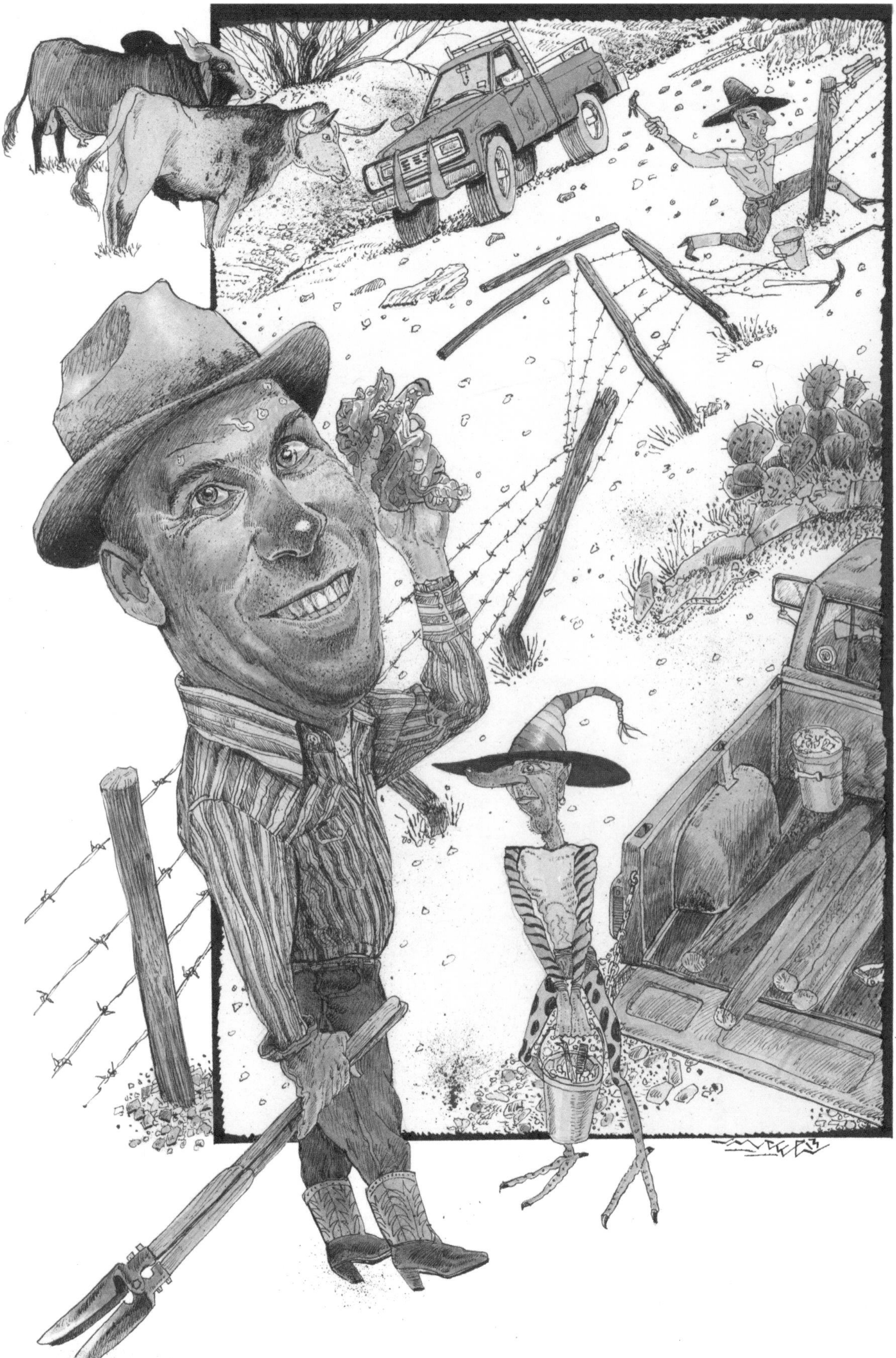

Q: If two ranches are separated by a length of old barbed-wire fencing and that fence needs repair, who is responsible come fence-mending time?
NAME WITHHELD, WEATHERFORD

A: Your inquiry is more well-timed than perhaps you know. It was 130 years ago this very summer that the Fence Cutting War broke out, a conflict pitting the state's landholding ranchers, who had begun to aggressively cordon off their property after the introduction of barbed wire in the 1870s, against its landless cowpunchers, who clung fiercely to the (less and less open) open range. When a severe drought made access to water and grass even more difficult, the free rangers began roaming about with wire cutters, wreaking havoc; the ranchers fought back. After the dust settled (literally—it being a drought, there was a lot of actual dust), the nipping of fence wire had been made a felony offense in Texas. But you came to the Texanist for counsel about the upkeep and repair of a common fence between two ranches, not a history lesson. The question, of course, is whether the fence is truly common or if its provenance can be established by reference to old documents, land surveys, and so on. But really, what fence between two spreads is not common? In the case of ranches, or any sort of adjoining property, one cannot build a fence, or any sort of boundary, without benefiting one's neighbor, even if one doesn't want to benefit one's neighbor because one's neighbor is an ornery old cuss. Such fences are, by their very nature, shared objects, though their purpose is to divide. But you came to the Texanist for maintenance advice, not armchair philosophy. In truth, though, it is exactly these sorts of historical and philosophical digressions that account for how long it can take some ranchers to get things done. The Texanist can picture a pair of them, standing out in their respective pastures, staring at a tangled heap of barbed wire, scratching their respective heads as they silently mull the mysteries of life and the two pertinent factors at play: "Do I have anything that needs a-fencin' in?" and "Does he have anything that needs a-fencin' out?" The Texanist's favored scenario has both men answering themselves in the affirmative, quickly shaking hands, and thus sealing a deal whereby the costs and labor will be split down the middle. ★

Q: I was born and raised in Texas and have resided in New York City for the past couple of years. On a recent trip back home, I visited a friend on his ranch in West Texas and was mocked unmercifully for wearing skinny jeans. I will admit that the jeans were pretty skinny. But from the reaction I got, you would have thought I was wearing a tutu and a pair of elf boots. Have rural Texans always been this closed-minded, or did I get what I deserved?

CALE BENNET, NEW YORK

A: The Texanist is a little bit surprised that the reaction you incited with your big-city style has left you in such a state of shock. Did you really think that your fancy pants would fly in West Texas without eliciting derisive commentary from the locals? In Austin, where the Texanist lives, the skinny-jeaned populace is sizable enough that these creatures can roam freely about the city without much notice (or as freely as the skintight denim of their sausage-casing-like dungarees allows). This is surely also the case on the fashion-forward streets of Gotham. But it's a much different story in the Texas hinterlands, where fashion is not forward—or leftward, rightward, or even backward. Those parts of the state are known to approve of a form-fitting jean when worn by a female (see "Tight Fittin' Jeans," by Conway Twitty; "Baby's Got Her Blue Jeans On," by Mel McDaniel; and other similar examples), but when the wearer is a man, the people out there do tend to lean, somewhat en masse, toward a more generous fit. Once upon a time the parameters for acceptability began and ended with the Wrangler 13MWZ Cowboy Cut, a style so prevalent as to have been officially sanctioned by the Professional Rodeo Cowboys Association in 1974. Nowadays, the variety of accepted looks has expanded—slightly. (Fun fact: just last year the PRCA updated its list of officially sanctioned jeans to include the new Wrangler 20X Collection Competition model, aka the 01MWX, which, in a sign of the times, features a cellphone pocket.) But as you surely know, West Texans remain a traditional folk in many regards, right down to the cladding of their lower halves. And since many of them are in the business, literally, of keeping the herd together, they are hardwired to take notice of mavericks and round them up. It appears that you may have pegged yourself as just such a maverick, sartorially speaking, and that your hosts, having spied you out there all alone in your skinny jeans, were only trying to get you back with the pack. ★

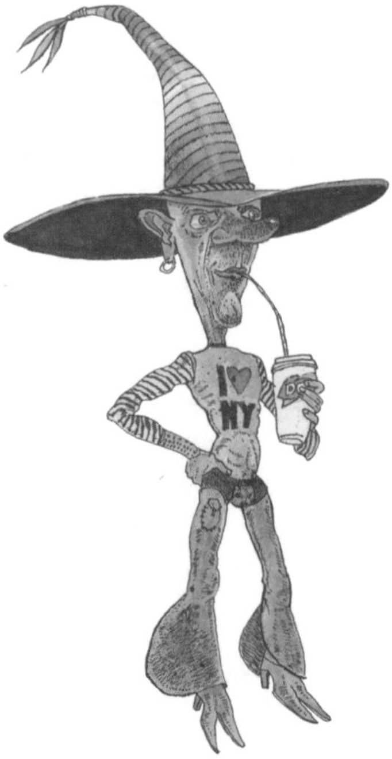
I ♥ NY

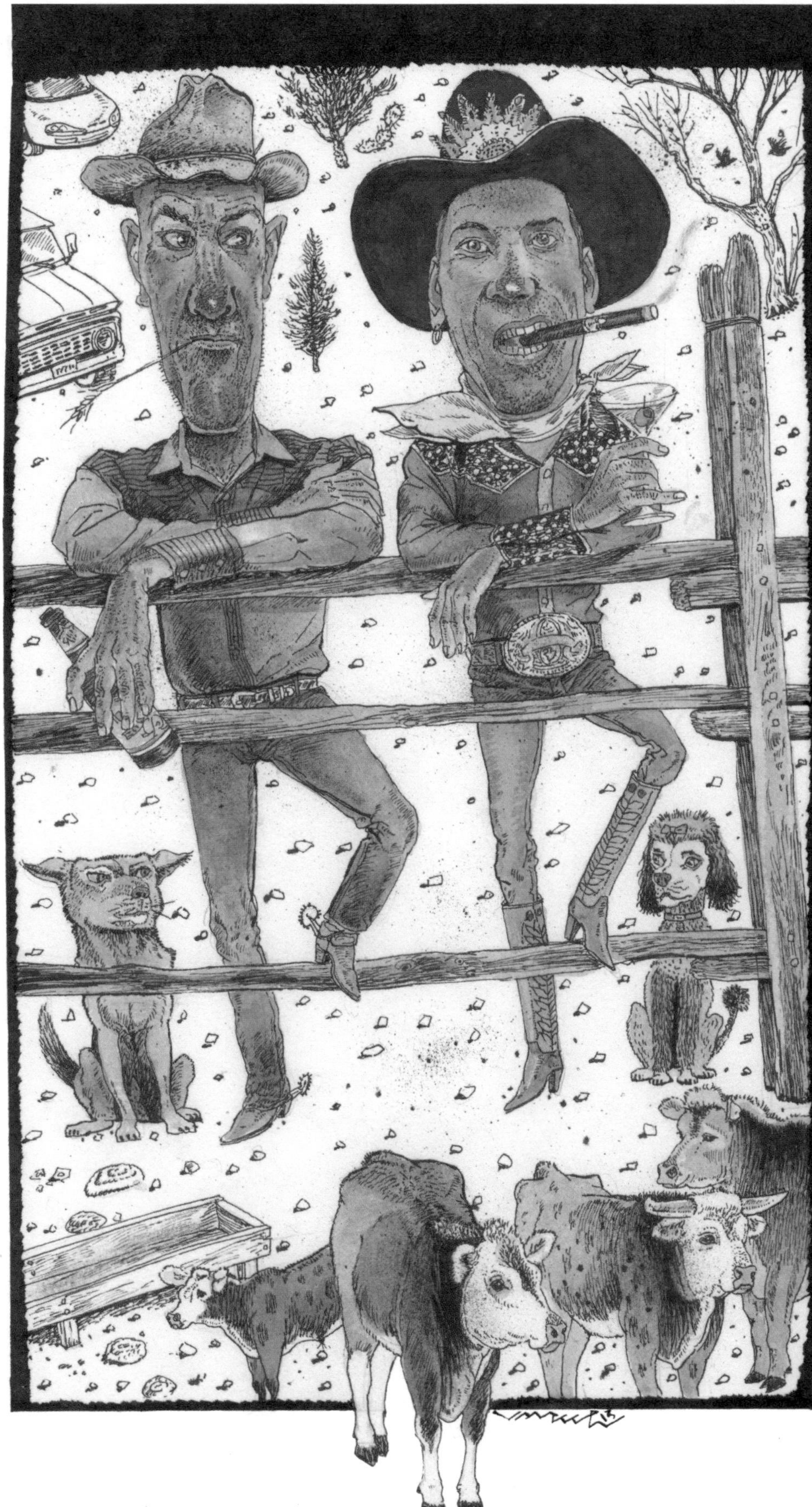

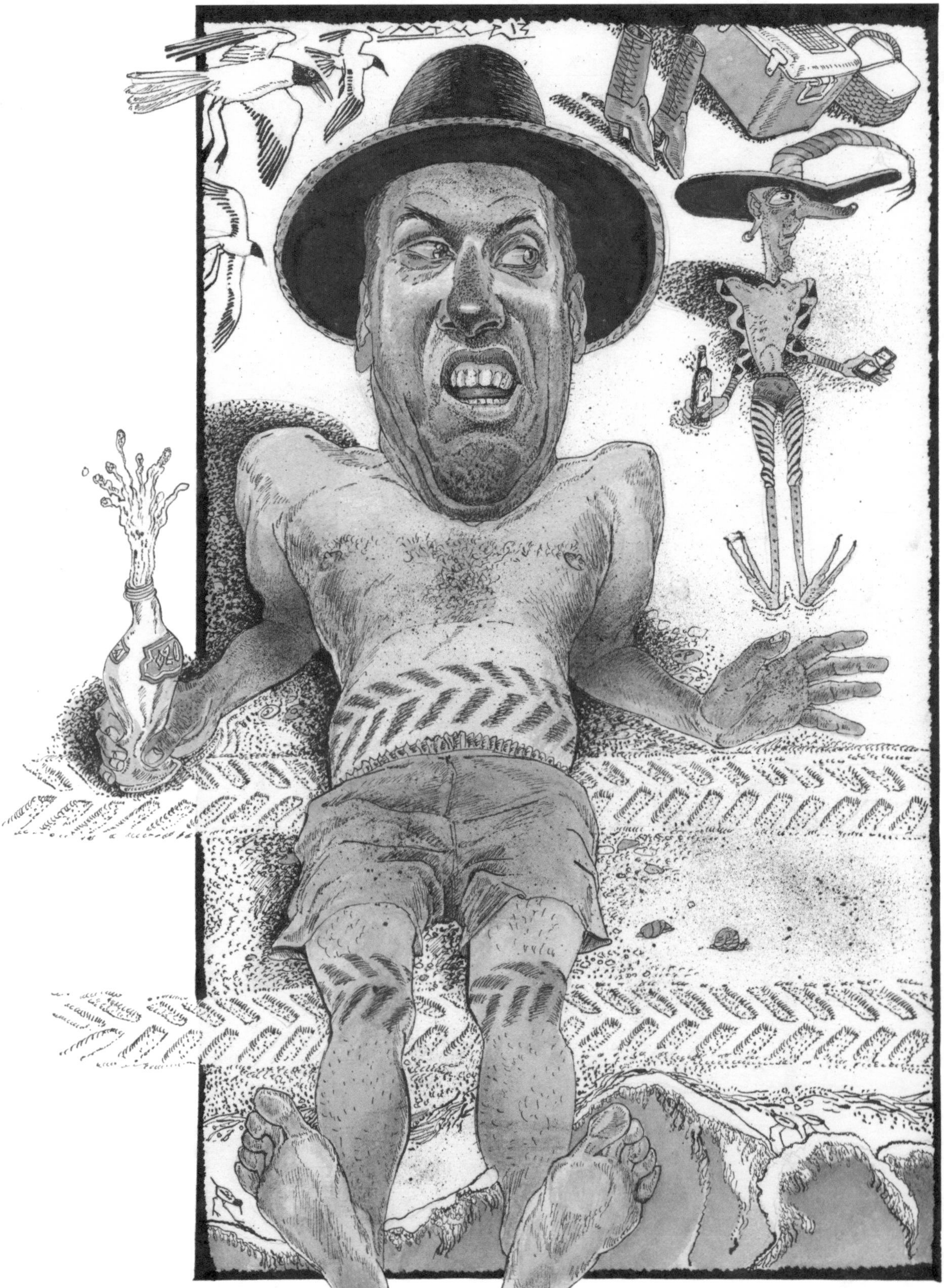

Q: I live in Arkansas but recently visited Port Aransas with my family for our summer vacation. We had never been to the Texas coast and were really looking forward to the trip, but it turned out that what could have been four beautiful days on the beach was marred by all the traffic! On the beach! Why on earth is driving allowed on Texas beaches? It's not safe.
THE PORTERS, LITTLE ROCK, ARKANSAS

A: The Texanist is glad that the Porters were able to escape their home in landlocked Arkansas and enjoy themselves on a nice stretch of the long, sun-drenched, and beautiful Texas coastline. There's nothing quite like the restorative effects of that salty Gulf air on both the body and soul, as you are now surely aware. Did you kick off your shoes and let that fine Texas sand work its warm magic on the old dogs as you reclined in your beach chair, sipping a koozie-clad Mexican beer with a little salt and a wedge of lime, while the white gulls cawed to one another and the brown pelicans soared in formation overhead and the sandpipers skittered nervously along the edge of the softly undulating surf? Cures what ails you, doesn't it? Speaking of the local fauna, it sounds like, in addition to these seabirds, you may have also been treated to a few sightings of the common Texas beach yahoo. These colorful beasts owe their existence, in part, to the Texas Open Beaches Act, passed in 1959, which at its core guarantees that "the public, individually and collectively, shall have the free and unrestricted right of ingress and egress to and from the state-owned beaches bordering on the seaward shore of the Gulf of Mexico." It's important to note here that the state owns the entirety of Texas's 367-mile coastline and that while some of the aforementioned public do indeed opt to make their ingresses and egresses vehicularly, the beach yahoo stands out by accenting his arrivals and departures with a signature yell and a couple of engine-roaring, sand-spewing doughnuts. The beach yahoo can be a dangerous bird, especially when in close proximity to young family members, and your outrage is understandable. It's also worth noting that the Open Beaches Act leaves the particulars of "public access" up to local jurisdictions along the coast and that some of them have opted to disallow vehicles from motoring upon the seashore. Such serene settings do not make good habitat for the yahoo, and it is generally found there only if it has become lost. The Porters ought to consider this when planning their next Texas getaway. ★

Q: I was born in Austin and have lived here almost my whole life. My wife was born and raised in New Orleans. After we got married, I convinced her to move to Austin. She loves it here, but she suffers so severely from cedar fever every year that she's begun to talk about relocating to New Orleans. Can you recommend a cure for that pesky pollen? NAME WITHHELD, VIA E-MAIL, AUSTIN

A: Runny nose, itchy eyes, nasal congestion, incessant sneezing, clogged ears, sore throat, aches about the face and head, malfunctioning sense of smell, fatigue, general malaise, and that customary nonstop grumbling about all of the above? Welcome to the Edwards Plateau, home of *Juniperus ashei*, or ashe juniper, also known as mountain cedar or post cedar or Mexican juniper or Texas cedar or the more colloquial "&#@%%ing $*%#@& $*#@%!" During winter, when these abundant evergreens release their pollen, they become the bane of an otherwise sublime Hill Country existence. In addition to the noxious clouds of microspores responsible for your wife's annual infirmities, the trees are regularly accused of drinking up precious water, offering poor forage for livestock, and, in general, just sucking. But they also prevent soil erosion and can provide good habitat for wildlife, including the endangered golden-cheeked warbler and the much less endangered white-tailed deer. The fact is, ashe juniper has been a part of the Texas landscape for thousands of years, and despite yearly cries for the tree's total eradication by pitchfork-, torch-, and Kleenex-wielding mobs, it ain't going anywhere. So let's see what we can do about getting your better, if temporarily more miserable, half to stick around too. The remedial options include, but are not limited to, cocktails of over-the-counter and prescription-strength antihistamines, decongestants, corticosteroids, and anti-inflammatory drugs; there are also nasal irrigation techniques, submersion in mud, staying indoors, and "the bottle." Famous folklorist, Austinite, and cedar-allergy victim J. Frank Dobie was known to hightail it out of town during the polleniest time of year, which can span a few weeks to two months around December and January, depending on conditions. Maybe you and the helpmeet would both benefit if she were to institute a similar yearly respite—a breather, if you will. From the Big Sneezy to the Big Easy, you might say. Be careful, though, as the Crescent City comes with its own irritating allergens. The Texanist once experienced a particularly severe reaction to the innumerable daiquiris, Sazeracs, and Pat O'Brien's Hurricanes he consumed on a night there—but he digresses. Gesundheit to you both. ★

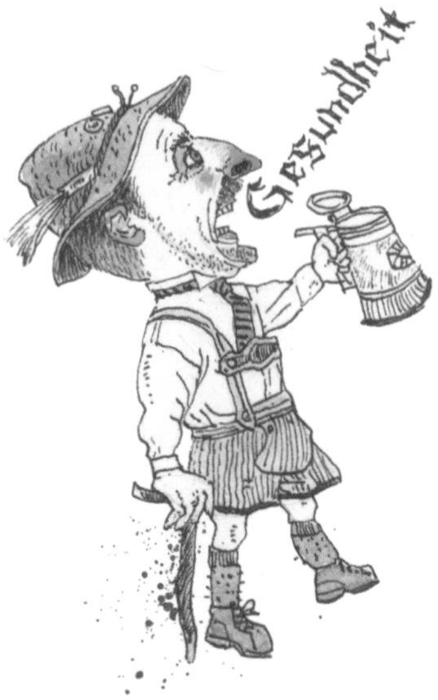
Gesundheit

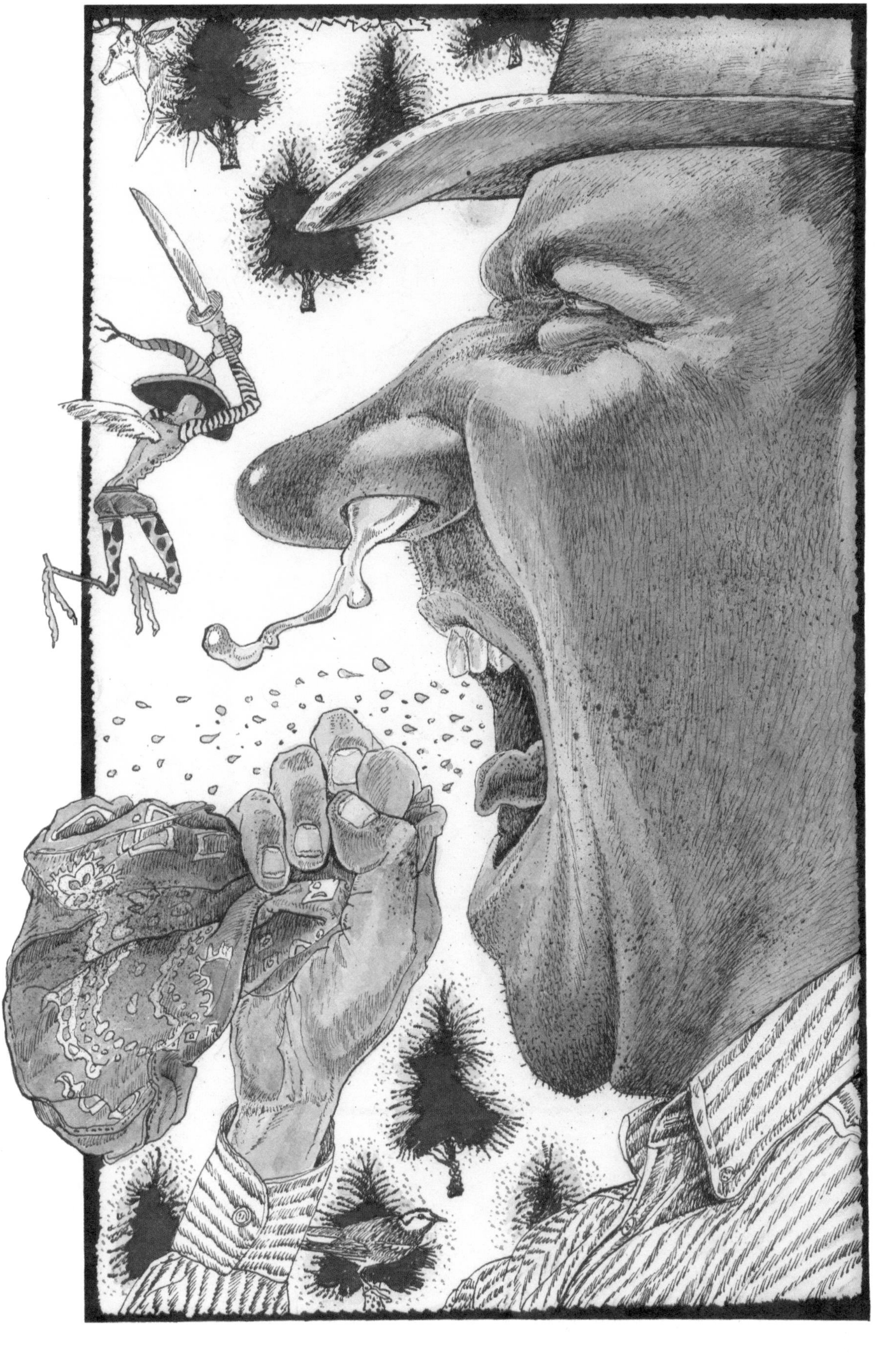

Q: My husband and I were recently visiting his parents' ranch in Central Texas when he started getting frisky with me one afternoon. The thing is, we were in a smelly barn. He apparently has some kind of fantasy involving "rolling in the hay." I told him that was just a euphemism and not meant to be taken literally. He was having none of it, insisting that there is something appealing about the idea of making love on an itchy pile of hay in a dirty barn. Texanist, please tell my husband that nobody actually "rolls" in hay.
NAME WITHHELD, AMARILLO

A: Thank you for the dirty letter. Before we get started, the Texanist would ask any former Sunday school teachers of his, along with all young children and the infirm or faint of heart, to please excuse themselves for a moment. Thank you. Now, pardon the Texanist for one more second while he knocks back a stiff belt. Ahem. Yes, these days a "roll in the hay" is, indeed, understood to be a euphemism for a casual and quick tryst that need not necessarily take place in a pile of hay. Before there were cars, or backseats of cars, or theater balconies, state park picnic tables, Dillard's dressing rooms, pickup-truck beds, no-tell motels, and the like, there was the hay. And the hay was as suitable a place as any for consenting couples to engage in impromptu copulative relations. The simple facts of life, in fact, inform us that for as long as humans have been cultivating, harvesting, and storing grasses for the purpose of nourishing their livestock, men and women have "rolled" in those stored grasses for the purpose of feeding the innate sexual appetites that roil within. An attraction to "the hay" is, for this reason, ingrained. And reminders of times when it was more frequently rolled in abound. Who, for instance, hasn't glimpsed a farm-implement manufacturer's wall calendar, hung behind the counter of the local feed store, featuring an image of a nubile young woman in a revealingly unbuttoned gingham blouse and a tiny pair of Daisy Duke shorts, gazing out with a come-hither look from a pile of hay in a rustic barn on a hot day? The Texanist knows he has. In the vast pantheon of graphic imagery that objectifies women, the proverbial farmer's daughter, almost always pictured in or near some hay, sits right up there with the sexy schoolteacher, the sexy librarian, and the sexy nurse. Human progress has, of course, given us a number of superior alternatives to the hay, which has caused it to fall out of favor among libidinous and determined young folk. But perhaps something deep inside your husband was awakened by the visit to the barn. Or perhaps he'd been to the feed store earlier that day. Whatever it was, he ended up with a serious case of "hay fever," for which the only cure was a "barn dance." Texas is one of the nation's top hay producers, and as such, there is often a lot of it lying around. When the conditions are right, some people, like your husband, will still want to "roll" in it. Without qualm. This is natural. Just put a blanket down first. That hay is mighty scratchy. ★

Q: On a recent trip to the Texas coast, my grown sons got into a heated four-day discussion. My younger son developed a craving for barbecue, so his brother used his Texas Monthly BBQ Finder app to locate a nearby source. Unfortunately, there wasn't one, and that's when the fight broke out. Younger son didn't care if a place wasn't on the list; he just wanted barbecue, comparing it to the old line, "There is no bad pizza." Older son refused to eat anywhere that wasn't on the list. It was the longest vacation ever. WWTTD: What would the Texanist do? NAME WITHHELD, ATOKA, OKLAHOMA

A: The Texanist is sorry that your vacation was so fraught with intrafamilial turmoil, but such are the passions aroused by barbecue. Like the impetuous younger brother in this meaty melodrama, the Texanist also used to stubbornly adhere to the belief that there is no such thing as bad barbecue. But that was a long time ago. Between those devil-may-care-what's-on-the-plate-so-long-as-it's-got-lots-of-sauce-on-top-of-it days, when the Texanist was but a wide-eyed young buck with horizons that lay not much beyond the outskirts of his hometown of Temple, and the present day, there have just been too many unpleasant encounters to carry on with an overoptimistic charade like this. The Texanist is here to tell you (and your younger son) that there is, unfortunately, such a thing as bad barbecue, and he knows this because he has ingested it. It may not be easy for the lad to swallow this bad news all at once, but he'll understand this unfortunate fact of life very clearly the first time a sliced Spam-like "brisket" substance is served to him off a dirty electric griddle by an old woman with long whiskers and grimy fingernails, like it once was at a joint outside Ozona. The Texanist, who was dining on the go, took one bite, placed the putrid stuff back in the bag, and then trepidatiously glanced at it there on the passenger-side floorboard all the way to Comstock, where it was disposed of. But he digresses.

So, is it better to risk an encounter with inedible barbecue or to go without barbecue altogether? Even knowing, as he now does, that the possibility of a truly horrific barbecue experience is real, little brother would probably choose the former, while big brother, the barbecue idealist in the family, would likely choose the latter, opting instead for a nearby Olive Garden. When a man has a hankering for some barbecue and there is no Texas Monthly BBQ Finder app–rated barbecue around, these are the options with which he is left. What would the Texanist do, you ask? Always a gambling man, the Texanist will roll the barbecue bones every time. ★

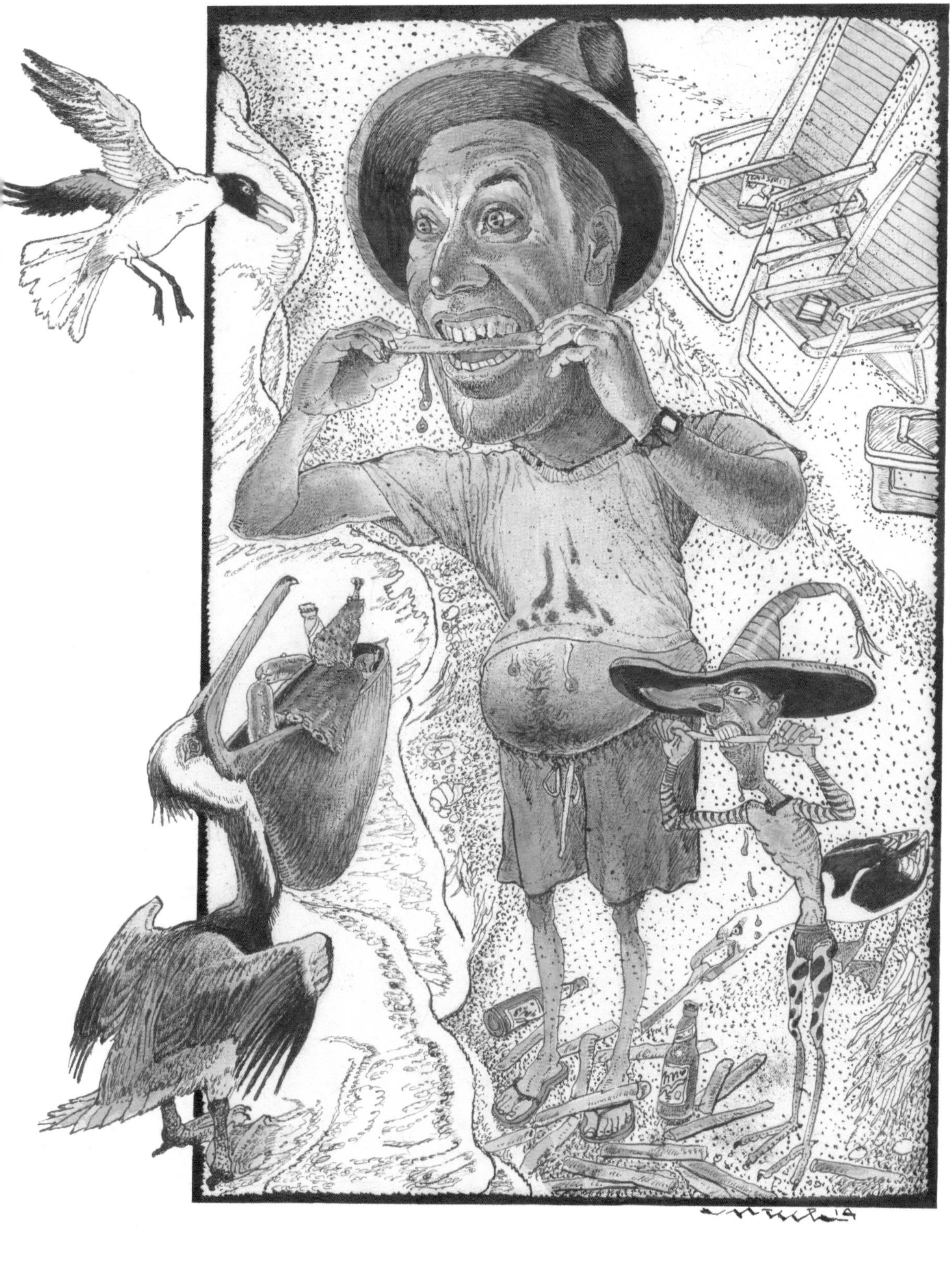

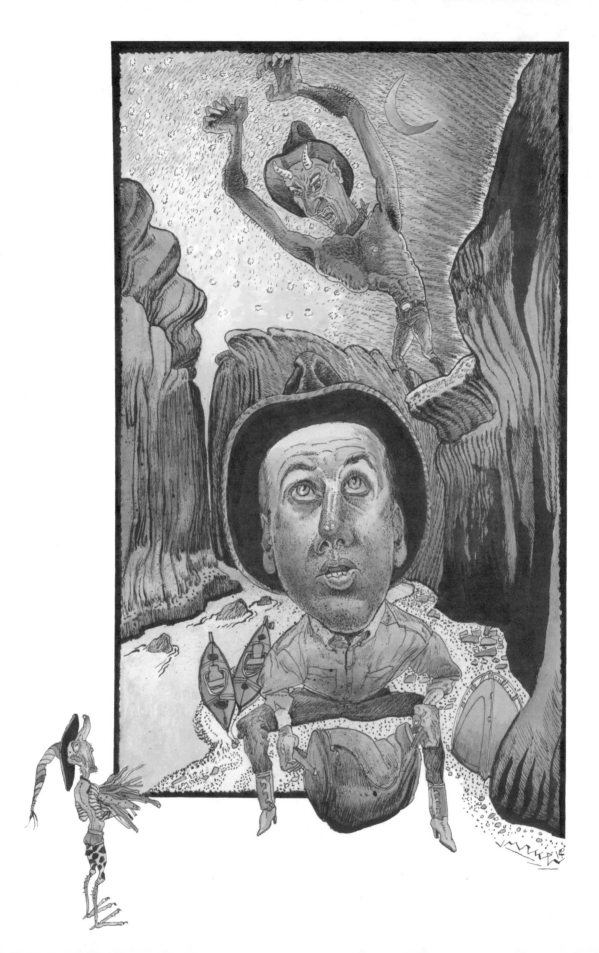

Q: My friends and I were paddling the Devils River in Val Verde County last spring. We drank some beer, we spilled our gear, and before we knew it, it was getting dark and we hadn't found a good island to camp on. So we pitched a tent on the bank below a bluff. Or at least we'd started to, when the owner of said bluff appeared and loudly informed us that we were on his property and needed to get lost. I know the navigable waters of Texas belong to all Texans, but I thought the banks of a stream were fair game too, since the water sometimes flows over them. Where did I go wrong? Or did I?
NATE B. SPOONER, AUSTIN

A: The Devils River is prized by paddling enthusiasts for its ruggedness, remoteness, and crystalline pristineness. Additionally, it has been known for the orneriness and occasional gun-totingness of the landowners through whose idyllically craggy properties this demonic yet handsome snake wends its way. As the Devils is bounded almost entirely by these private lands, making camp can pose problems. Islands in the stream offer a good option for an overnight (as well as for one hell of a Kenny Rogers and Dolly Parton duet) if, as they say, the good Lord is willing and the river don't rise, which it sometimes very rapidly does. But even the best-laid plans can be affected by a fast-setting sun, paddle-weary muscles, and a beckoning cooler full of ice-cold beer. Clearly this is what happened on your trip.

The navigable waters of Texas do indeed belong to all Texans. And so do the streambeds upon which they flow. The problem is that the exact line demarcating the parts of the streambed belonging to the public and the parts belonging to private parties, a border known as the gradient boundary, is not always an obvious one. The Supreme Court of Texas has defined the streambed as the "soil which is alternately covered and left bare as there may be an increase or diminution in the supply of water, and which is adequate to contain it at its average and mean stage during an entire year, without reference to the extra freshets of the winter or spring or the extreme droughts of the summer or autumn"; further, the court has located the gradient boundary "midway between the lower level of the flowing water that just reaches the cut bank, and the higher level of it that just does not overtop the cut bank."

This information, pertinent though it may be, leaves the Texanist's head aswirl in an eddy of words, and an attempt to explain such a befuddlement to that landowner, with his nostrils flaring as they were, would most assuredly have been a fruitless endeavor. Ideally, river trips go according to plan, and camp is made without incident at a prearranged, legal spot. Occasionally, though, things do not go as planned. In these situations, it's the Texanist's hope that reasonable heads prevail. As you survived to write this letter, it appears to have worked out this way for you and your party. Congratulations. ★

Q: I am an avid player of Words With Friends. Although proper nouns are not allowed, the word "Texas" is accepted but the word "Texan" is not. How can this possibly be? I think this is a travesty that should be rectified.

DARLENE THOMPSON, LEAGUE CITY

A: If the Texanist were to sit down at his writing desk and jot down all the various pastimes with which he has been known to while away the hours in avoidance of his deadlines, playing Words With Friends on his mobile telephone would certainly appear on that list, alongside whittling, skipping stones, challenging the interns to rounds of mumblety-peg, and a whole slew of other entertaining inanities. He too considers himself an avid player, although his editor, wife, daughter, golf buddies, family dog, and person behind him in the drive-through line at the bank would probably choose a different descriptor on those occasions when the Texanist is hunched over in that glowy-faced WWF trance, unmoving.

For the Luddites out there, Words With Friends is similar to the classic board game Scrabble, and it just happens to have been created right here in Texas by a McKinney-based game company. The game's list of acceptable words is based on the Enhanced North American Benchmark Lexicon and currently contains more than 173,000 possible entries. But you are right in your observation with regard to the "Texas" anomaly and the unacceptability of proper nouns. Your view, however, that the omission of "Texan" is a bunch of BS is not completely defensible. ("BS," by the way, when spelled out, is an acceptable word, as is "cowpie," one that always brings a smile to the Texanist's face when he has the opportunity to play it.) It turns out that there is an alternative definition of "Texas" that is not a proper noun: A "texas" is a structure on a steamboat that houses the officer's cabins. So while "Texan" is an unacceptable Words With Friends word, "texas" (or "taxes," if you'd rather) will earn you a few points. Similarly, "alaska" (as in baked alaska) and "colorado" (a shade of cigar) are acceptable as well as both "new" and "jersey" (as long as they are not used in conjunction). Now, if you'll please excuse the Texanist, it's his move in a lively match he's got going with his 11-year-old daughter. She just dropped "jodhpurs" on him for huge points, and he has nothing but a tray full of vowels. ★

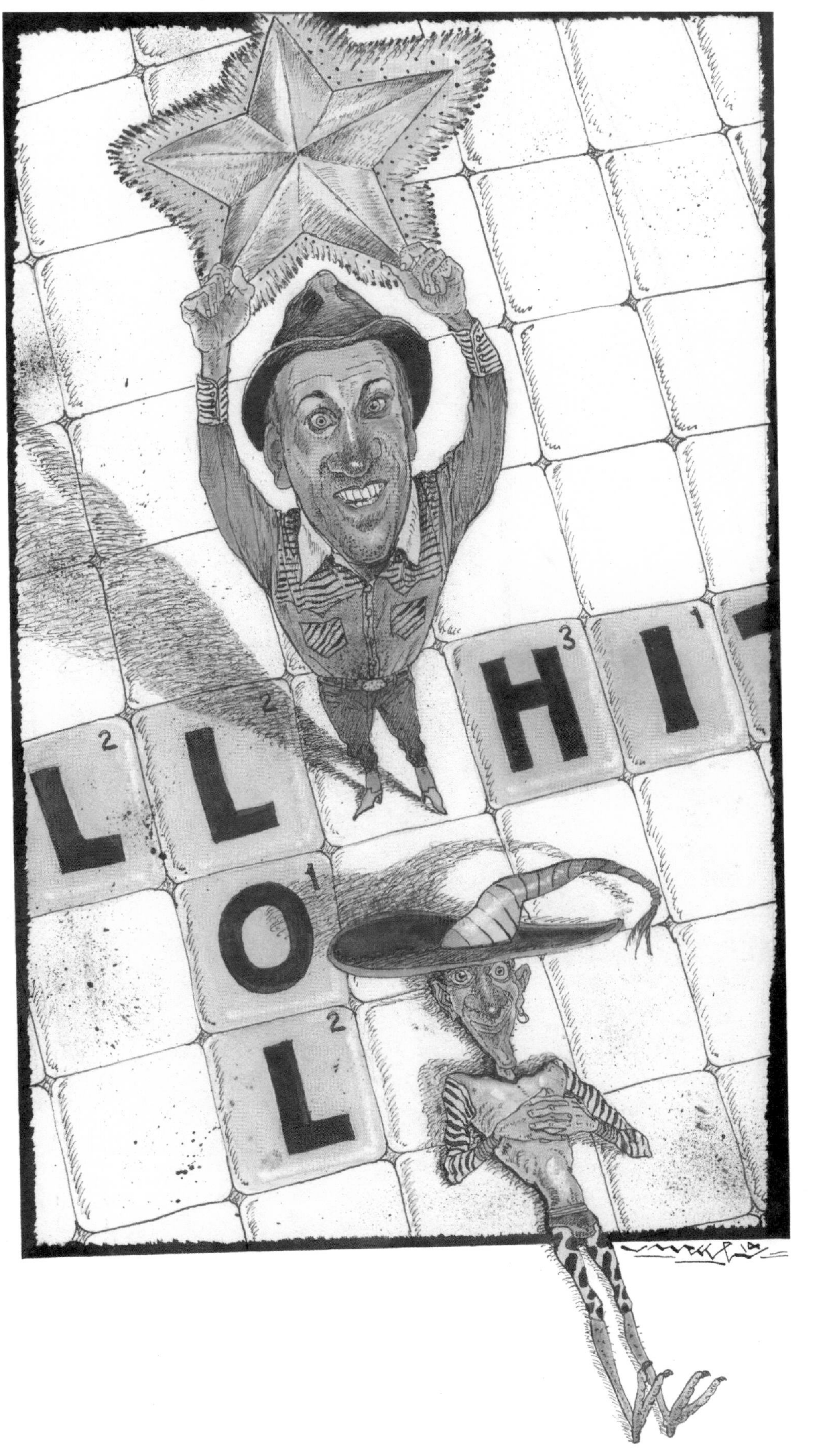
LLHIT
O
L

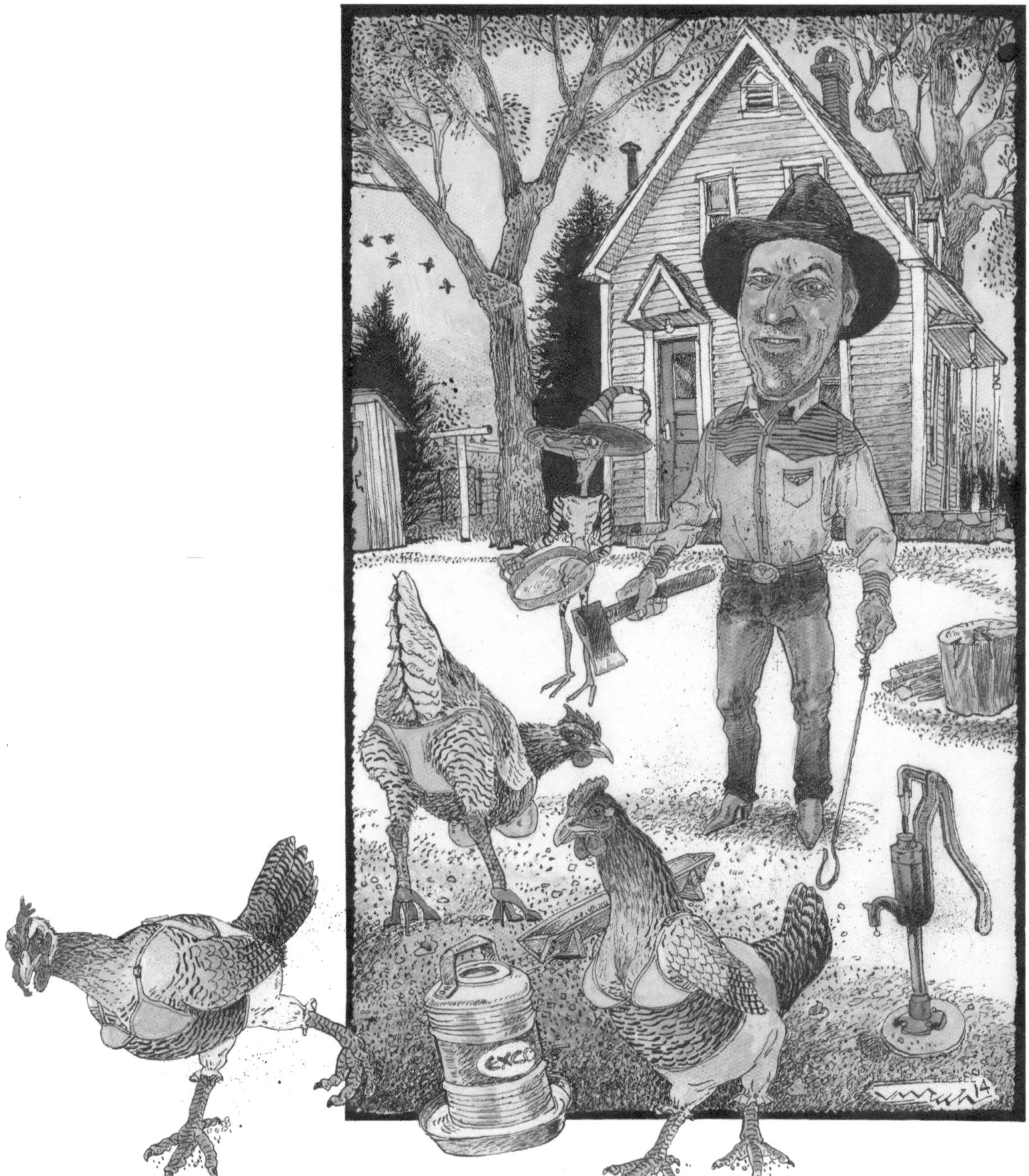

Q: During my boyhood years, I would spend time at my father's family farm, near Sardis, in Ellis County. The main meal was at noon and often featured fried chicken, and we kids wound up with drumsticks, wings, or "second joints." It wasn't until later that I learned a second joint was also called a "thigh." I assume the shift was meant to be more decorous, since we also NEVER said "breast" but only "white meat." Were these circumlocutions widespread? NORMAN ROE, CEDAR PARK

A: Euphemisms for poultry parts deemed to be unmentionable in mixed company were indeed once more commonly heard around the dinner table than they are these days—especially throughout the South, where manners, like Bibles and delicious homemade fried chicken, were much more ubiquitous than they are today. The logic behind such rebranding, while under the guise of general politeness, actually had to do with the prudish and some-times completely dead-on assumption that any edible part of an animal that carried an ana-tomical place-name that could be matched to a corresponding body part on the human form would prove to be too tempting for pent diners to avoid fixating upon. But even without the shield of white meats, dark meats, drumsticks, and second joints there to protect the par-ticularly hell-bound among us from the large and juicy breasts; the lean, muscular legs; and the mysteriously tempting tenders, it's highly unlikely that everybody at the table would have gone goo-goo-eyed as the meal devolved into a depraved, orgiastic mess the first time Uncle Carl was heard to say, "Let me grab one of those fine-looking breasts there, will you?" Even the advent of the horseless carriage, the radio, the television, the JC Penney catalog lingerie section, fast food, and the Internet have yet to bring about humanity's end—although the music the Texanist is forced to listen to on the way to his daughter's school in the mornings has him pondering the actual proximity of the end-times more and more. Thing is, Mr. Roe, there is no way to know exactly how prevalent these morally superior–seeming code names for chicken parts were. But it's a fact that they are heard less now than they were in the days of those trips to the cloistered safety of your daddy's family farm. ✶

Q: I have been receiving *Texas Monthly* as a gift subscription for about four years now. When a new issue arrives, I turn to the back to read your column first. There are usually several laughing matters contained therein. But my son and I often discuss the picture of your little friend, the one with the multicolored sombrero and chicken feet—the little guy always at your side, the one out on a limb for you, carrying the load. Pray, after all this time, tell us more about your miniature sidekick. DEBBY HOLT, GRAPEVINE

A: The Texanist typically advises against seeing how the "sausage" is made. And the assembly of advice sausage can be particularly messy. But as the focus of your inquiry is this most-unsung creature, a tip of the hat to him by way of a quick peek behind the curtain is, after all these years, probably warranted. Ever since this column made its debut, way back in the summer of 2007, it has been accompanied by the colorfully illustrative creations of Dallasite Jack Unruh, an artiste nonpareil in yours truly's humble opinion. And there, in the very first installment that July, like a fluttering spirit guide summoned by the Texanist in the balmy, smoky, and peyote-fueled weirdness of a medicinal sweat lodge, was the man-handed, chicken-footed, big-nosed, sometimes-winged, oft-bedraggled one known around the office as Li'l Bubba, or sometimes, "that strange wizard-lizard thing in the leopard-print tights with the creepy facial expressions." From that point forward, the little fella has appeared in these many, many columns as half of a dynamic duo charged with bettering our countrymen and countrywomen via the signature fine advice found on these pages each month. When that guy from Mabank wanted to know, in April 2012, what was the deal with "truck balls," it was Li'l Bubba who offered his trademark rainbow-colored chapeau as a receptacle while the Texanist, in a demonstration of his disapproval of such automotive accoutrements, castrated a truck. And that one time last January, when a certain "Name Withheld" wondered whether it was a good idea to let a teenage son attend a coed campout, it was the same Li'l B who could be seen fencing off a young Texanist from his female camping companion. In short, Li'l Bubba is Deputy Fife to the Texanist's Sheriff Taylor, Cato Fong to his Inspector Clouseau, Trigger to his Roy Rogers, and Babilonia to his Gardner. Simply put, this column would have a much harder time serving its intended purpose without him. So let us now raise a glass to Li'l Bubba and, by extension, to the inimitable Jack Unruh. Hear, hear! Thanks for the question. And thanks, too, to the generous soul who has supplied you with the long-renewed gift subscription. ★

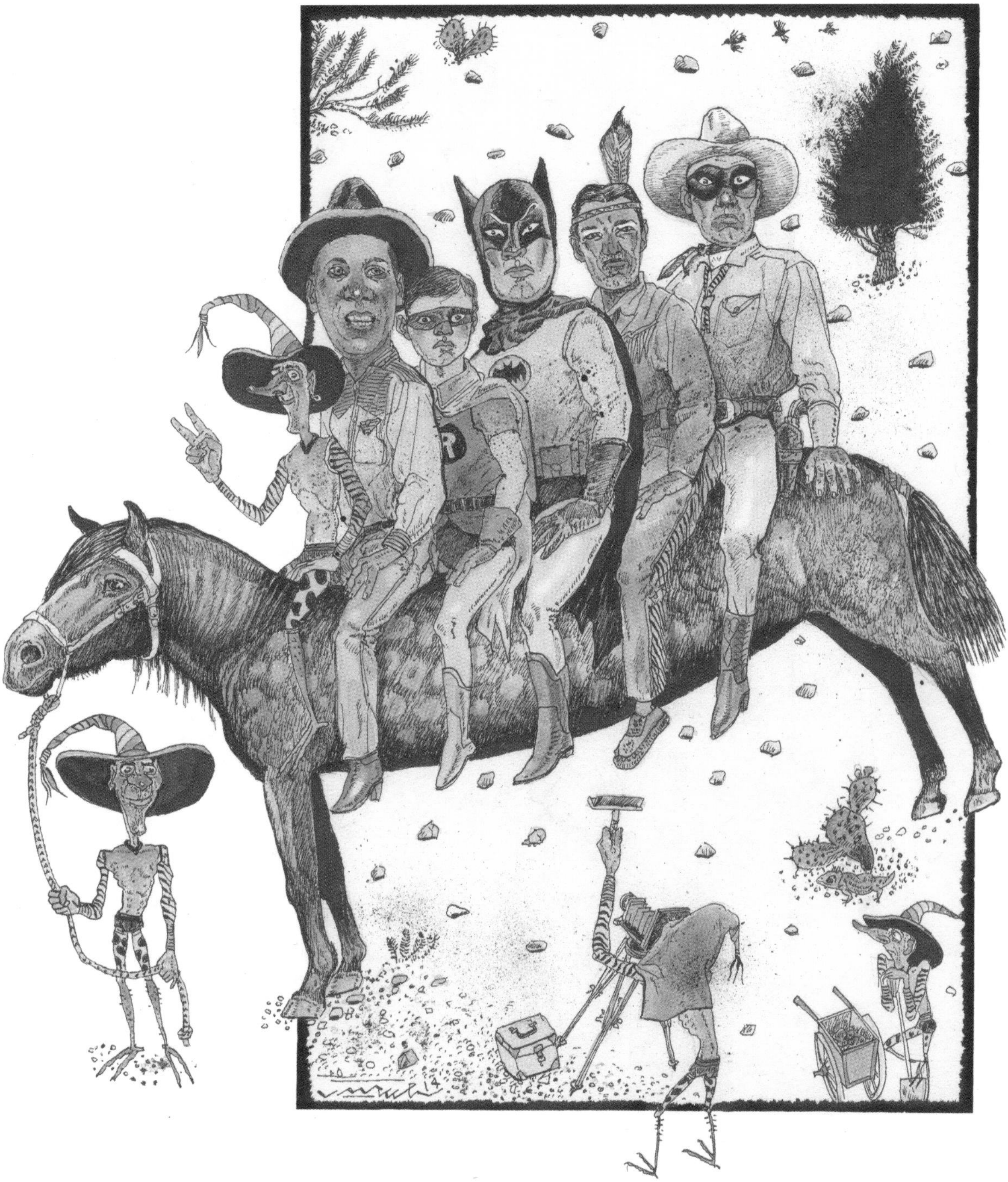

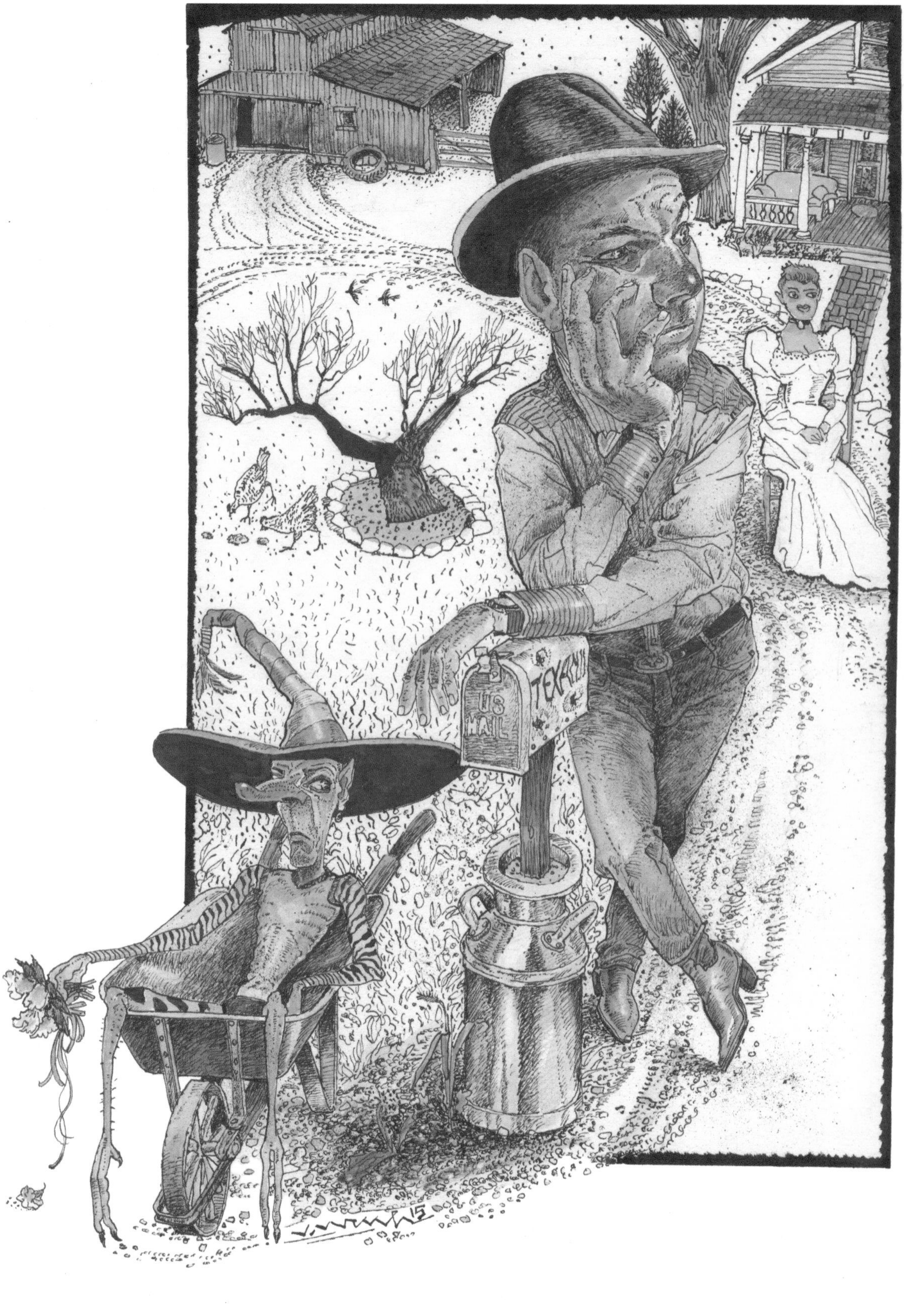
US MAIL

Q: A few months ago I was flying out of the Austin airport on the way to my honeymoon. As I reached the front of the security line, I realized that I had mistakenly left my pocketknife—a gift from my new bride—in my carry-on bag. My only options were trashing it or using an automated kiosk, run by a company in North Carolina, to have the knife mailed back to my house. I'll spare you the long, frustrating details, but suffice it to say, 83 days have passed, and I still haven't received my beloved knife. The company in question has offered little help. Can you? PAUL K., AUSTIN

A: The Texanist arms himself each morning from a drawerful of trusty pocketknives, among which are a number of sentimental favorites. He's got knives from his wife. He's got knives from his dad. He's got knives from his brother, his uncles, his aunts, his colleagues, and his friends. Indeed, it's a rare moment when he is caught without at least one of these cherished folding blades. The Texanist can only imagine what you must be going through. First the marriage, which makes for a big enough life-changing experience, and then, on top of that, you are stripped of your new pocket shank. How will the occasional dangling thread be pruned from your garments? With what will you whittle? Your mail will be tended to in a ham-fisted manner or just left on the counter unopened. Dear Lord, there's no time to waste. So, never one to advise standing idly by in the face of a wrongdoing, the Texanist has taken the liberty of firing off an angry letter for you. Fill in the blanks as you see fit and post at will.

Dear Sirs (a term I use loosely):

Apparently due to the heady effects of getting hitched just one day prior, I failed to properly secure the pocketknife that my brand-new bride had given me in my checked baggage as I normally would have, per TSA rules. Rather than forgoing the honeymoon flight so that I could run the knife back home myself, I chose—at the urging of my wife—to trust your company, for a slightly gougey fee I might add, with the knife's safe handling and prompt return.

Alas, you [fill in the blank] North Carolinian SOBs have failed to live up to your end of the [fill in the blank] deal for three [fill in the blank] months now! How the [fill in the blank] you [fill in the blank] can sleep at night is beyond me. Please return my [fill in the blank] pocketknife posthaste. Failure to comply could result in the full wrath of one quite [fill in the blank] irritated Mrs. Paul K. being rained down upon you for this gross bungling—much as it has rained down upon me ever since exiting that [fill in the blank] security line at the Austin airport. You have been warned!

Sincerely, Your Name Here

Whether this note gets results or not, the Texanist is certain that you'll feel better after having sent it. Ultimately, pocketknives are replaceable. Clear consciences and first wives are not. ★

Q: After eighteen years of exile in California, my wife and I were able to retire and move back home. One of our retirement dreams was to get a condo on South Padre Island—by far the best Texas beach. After visiting recently, we are reconsidering. The SPI that we remembered had a great beach, not one with so much vegetation. Can you recommend other Texas beaches that now rival the old SPI? CHUCK FOX, SAN ANTONIO

A: The Texanist, a lifelong beachgoer, has been lucky enough to have spent time on a large variety of coasts. He's been on the East Coast, the West Coast, multiple Mexican coasts, and coasts across the pond too. The Texanist, it has been rightly said, is a salty man. But as you might have guessed, the majority of his saltiness comes from time spent along Texas's Gulf Coast, on the "Texas Riviera" in particular, just north of the Mansfield cut and just south of San José Island, at a spot where the Texanist's family has been visiting since the late sixties. Except for their proximities to the briny deep, none of these sandy places are exactly alike, and the Texanist is here to tell you that even the very same stretch of beach can change in appearance quite dramatically from one visit to the next. That's the thing about beaches: Because of the highs and lows of tidal influence, the some-times-blustery coastal winds, those ever-shifting sands, and the varying amounts of flotsam, jetsam, washed-up garbage, and smelly and unsightly—but ecologically healthy—seaweed that happen to be present at a particular time, all beaches are in a state of perpetual flux. One day it's a tropical paradise and the next it's a nasty-looking, intolerable hell. Unless your last trip happened to have coincided with a rowdy spring break, this phenomenon is probably the source of your divergent South Padre experiences. And, then, the Texanist also wonders if the eighteen years you spent in the Golden State haven't left your head overly sun-kissed and swimming with visions of those idyllic Annette Funicello and Gidget movies. Whatever the cause, you have misinterpreted the true potential of one of Texas's most perfectly suitable settings for a beachside retirement condominium. Instead of advising that you give Mustang Island or Galveston Island or Surfside Beach or the Bolivar Peninsula a try, the Texanist will instead suggest that you have another look at South Padre. You seem to have loved it once, and he's sure that you will once more. ⋆

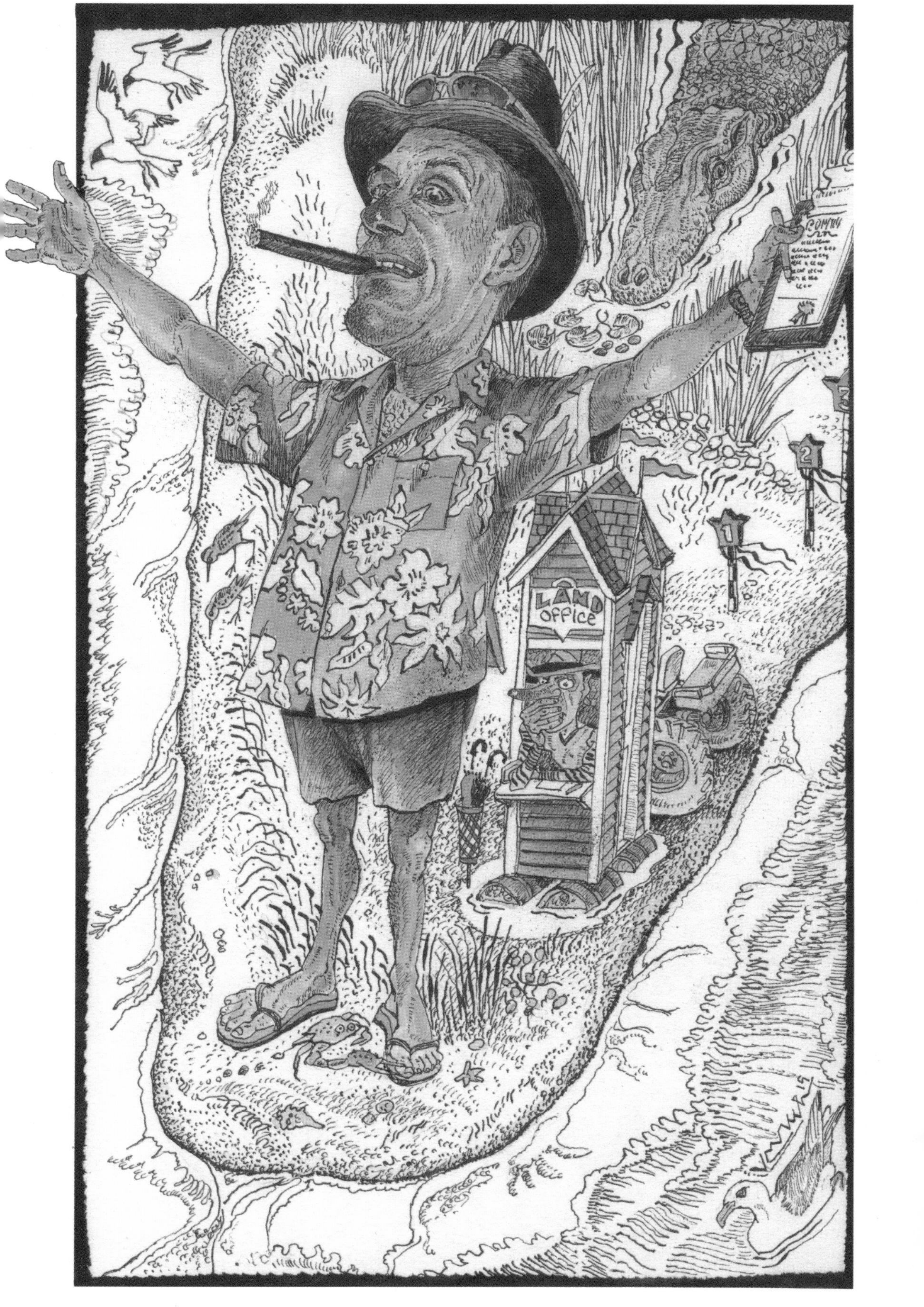
LAND
Office

Q: This spring I was driving from New Orleans to Austin, and a little west of Winnie it became obvious that some really bad weather lay ahead. By the time I was on Interstate 10, driving cautiously through a downpour near downtown Houston, I realized that I had no idea what I should do if I saw a tornado, which didn't seem too far-fetched, considering the weather alerts blowing up on my phone and the cloud formations. What should the prudent driver do, especially if exit ramps are far apart, making it difficult to legally (and safely) skedaddle in the opposite direction? JANIS DAEMMRICH, AUSTIN

A: Texas and the weather have an excellent relationship for the most part, as nearly any Texan will be happy to discuss with you in great detail. But as those same Texans will also be happy to discuss with you, the possibility of things turning suddenly rocky is an ever-present reality. One need only recall the events of this spring and summer for proof. There is a saying that goes, "If you don't like the weather in Texas, wait five minutes." It's an old and overused adage, and it's not always a reliable predictor of good weather, as sometimes five minutes pass and whoosh!—tornadic activity has ensued. This is exactly why it's not a bad idea to be familiar with the ins and outs, ups and downs, and round and rounds of safely riding out a bout of inclement weather here at the southern end of Tornado Alley. The Texanist will have you know that instead of disregarding weather warnings and blindly plowing headlong into the darkening yonder, travelers are urged to take heed of such alerts and seek sanctuary in the nearest sturdy structure. Although you managed to arrive at your destination intact, you will be especially relieved to know that a car (yes, even a truck) is about the least safe place to be in the event of a tornado. But when a person is caught out on the road, unable to skedaddle in the opposite direction or find a suitable haven, it is recommended that you not do your ducking and covering on the floorboard of your car (or truck). Rather, you are advised to abandon the vehicle, hunker down in the nearest ditch or ravine, and hope for the best. The Texanist will not quibble with the safety advice of the experts, but he would add that it also couldn't hurt, at such a harrowing point, to let loose with a long string of expletives or a heartfelt prayer to the higher power of your choice. ⋆

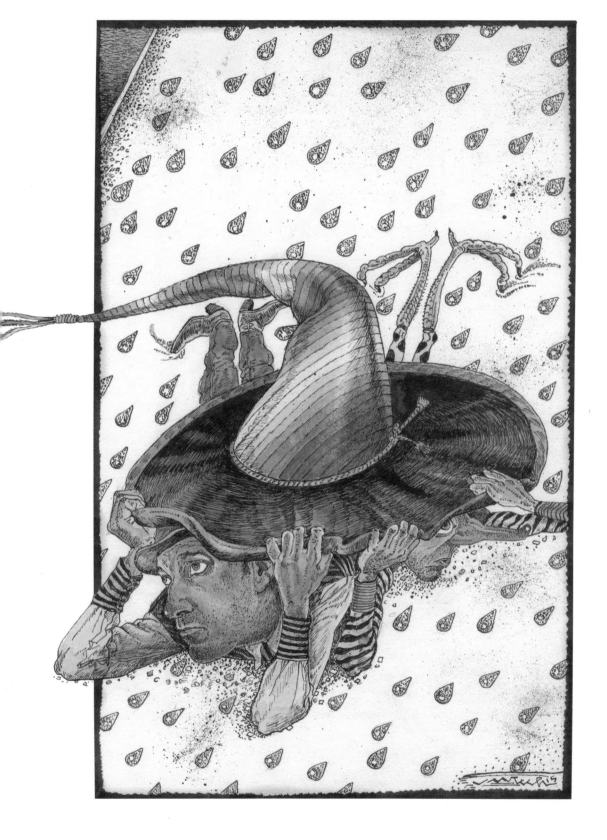

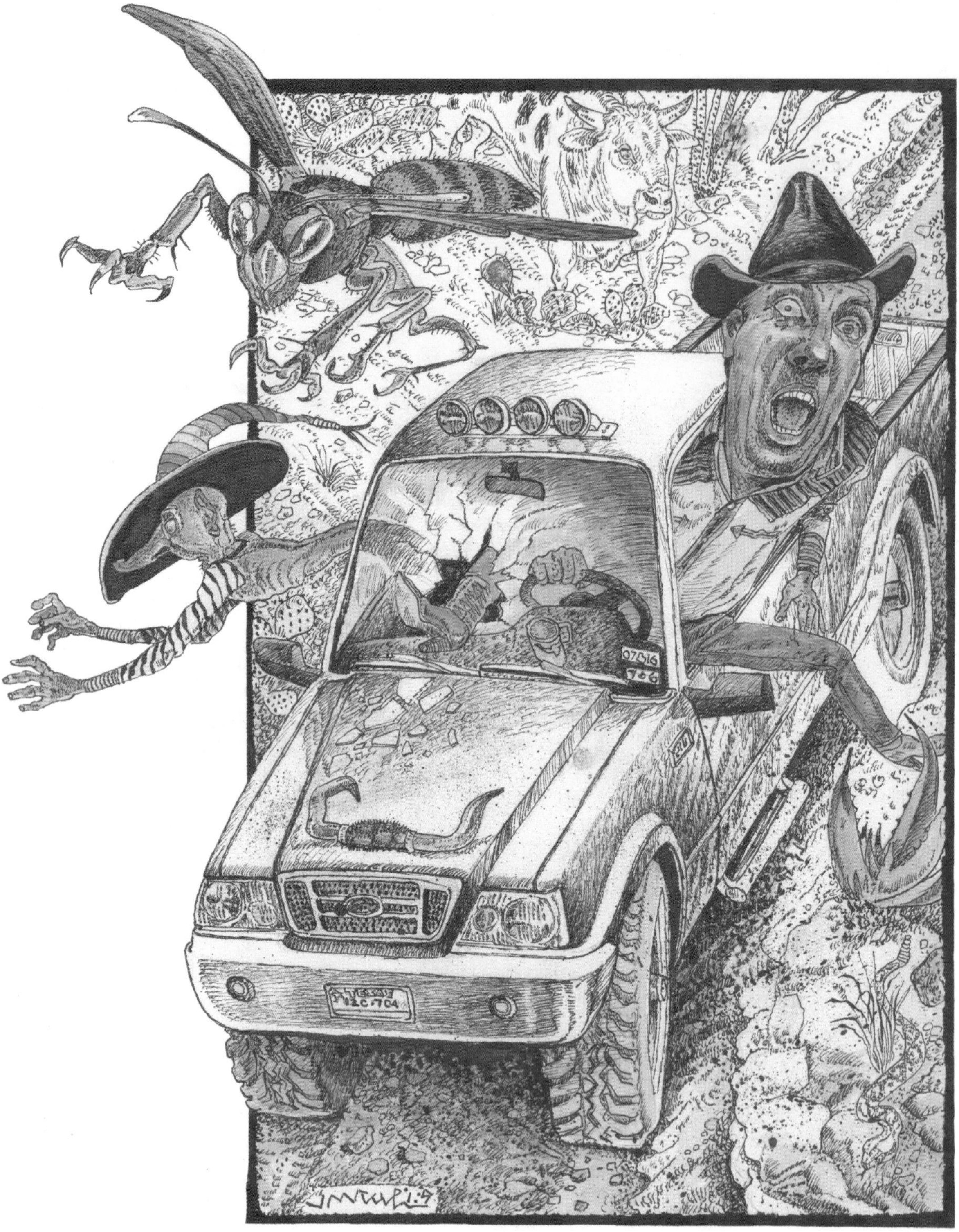

Q: While driving around a friend's ranch, my usually stoic buddy flipped down his visor and found that a red wasp had hitched a ride with us. All of a sudden he's like Janis Joplin being electrocuted. When the dust settled, I had been stung on the forehead and my friend had his foot stuck behind the steering wheel. So, just how should a proper Texan handle himself in the presence of a small stinging insect? Also, what is the statute of limitations on razzing him about his behavior? NAME WITHHELD, FORT WORTH

A: Unflinching stoicism in the face of terrifying obstacles is one of the most enduring characteristics of the mythic Texan. Think John Wayne at "the Alamo"; or Captains Call and McCrae out on the wild trail, where danger lurked behind every sage bush; or the Texanist's plucky missus after the Texanist, while out on the town, has pushed the boundaries of his Mexican martini consumption well past the point of public acceptability. As you see, the taming of this harsh land we call home often involved scrapes with dangerous and unsavory characters, and indeed, it still does. The red wasp is included among such risks, along with hornets, yellow jackets, bees, horseflies, and Mexican martinis. But while these red menaces of the porch eaves—known officially and somewhat less ominously as paper wasps—will typically attack only when they feel that their nest is in danger, the mere threat of the mighty(ish) wallop that is their sting is enough to send most folks into a state of discomposure, and then, depending on the closeness of the encounter, possibly into the spasmodic throes of a full-blown conniption fit, like the one you witnessed your friend have in the cab of the truck that day. His reaction, though, while perhaps a smidge melodramatic, was not really all that unusual for the circumstance. In fact, it is precisely this sort of wild thrashing and high-pitched childlike screaming that has kept many a Texan from getting stung by red wasps, which, if the Texanist recalls correctly, is exactly the opposite of what happened to you, on your forehead, as you calmly sat there like a slack-jawed lump on a log. As for an expiration date on ridiculing your friend, the Texanist advises caution in stirring this proverbial hornet's nest. The chance of suffering another welt on the forehead does exist. ⋆

Q: This past summer my teenage daughter and her friend tie-dyed some T-shirts in our garage, and now my husband has found me "complicit" in the "desecration" of his beloved chili pot, which he recently discovered had a remnant of dye in it. I fear that our 24-year-long relationship has been irreparably damaged. How can I make this right? NAME WITHHELD, SAN ANTONIO

A: The Texanist cooks his chili in the very same pot from which the meaty stew of his youth was long ago ladled. This prized vessel was handed down to him by his father, a fine man and pretty fair chili chef. Every time the Texanist cooks chili, he thinks of his dad. The pot is special to him. Thus, the Texanist can understand your husband's three-alarm disappointment as a result of the freaky goings-on in his own cherished pot. But the Texanist is also the father of a daughter who is prone to occasional mishaps, mostly of an innocent nature so far. By the Texanist's estimation, your husband, depending on the exact age of your girl, is somewhere between 13 and 18 years late in realizing that once a child enters the picture, few treasured personal items will, for one reason or another, retain their sacred status. That failed diaper that permanently stained the couch in his man cave and the sippy cup full of chocolate milk that was allowed to leak its entire contents down the crack of his truck's backseat only to be discovered a week later should have been the first of many clues. Since your husband's pot was not rendered inoperable by the tie-dying or really even all that desecrated, the Texanist finds you not guilty of complicity. But to help with the thawing of the chilliness between you and Mr. Name Withheld caused by this misadventure, simply wash the pot thoroughly and then have your husband reconsecrate it to its former perceived glory with a big batch of his "famous" Texas red. ★

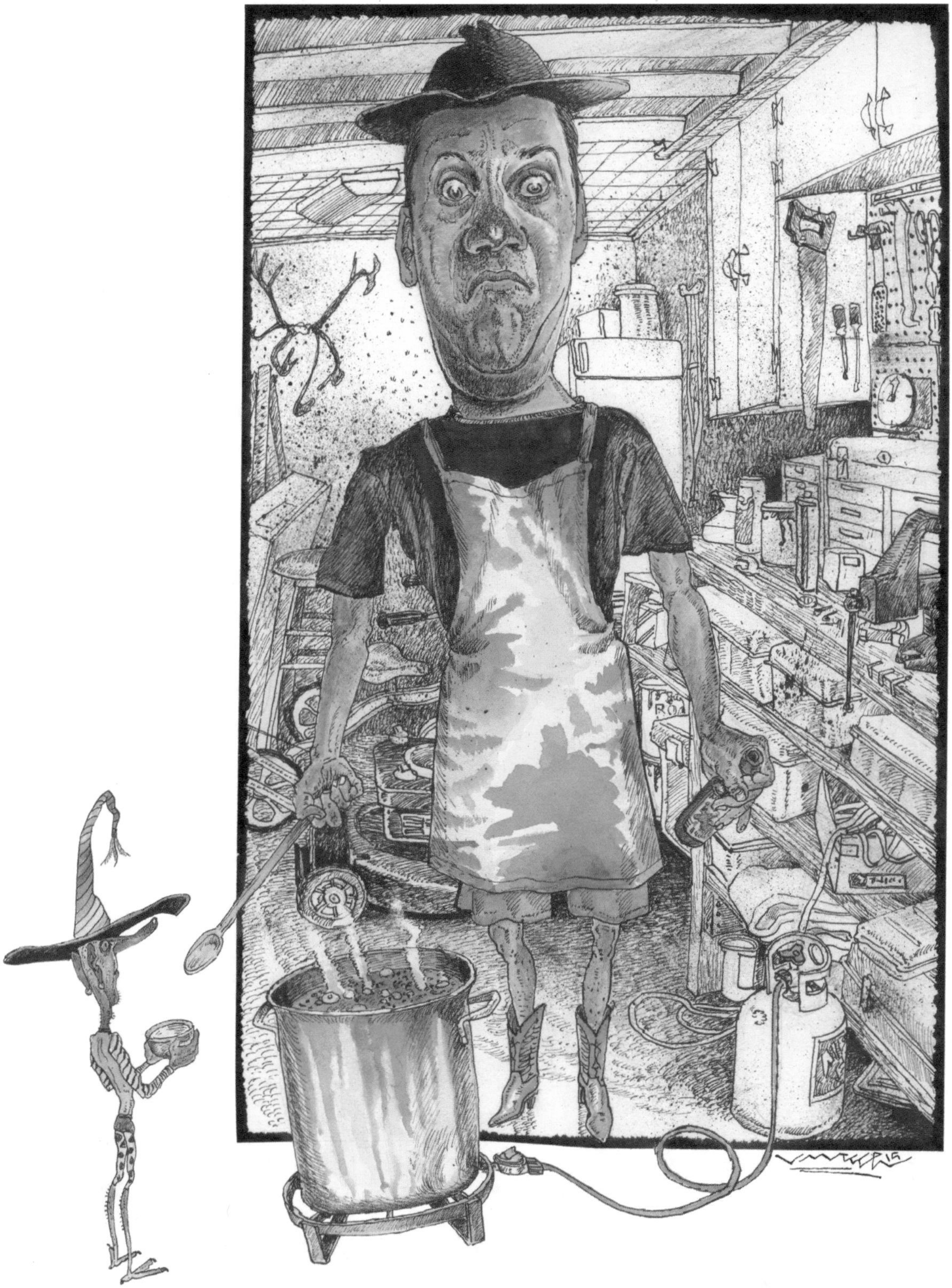

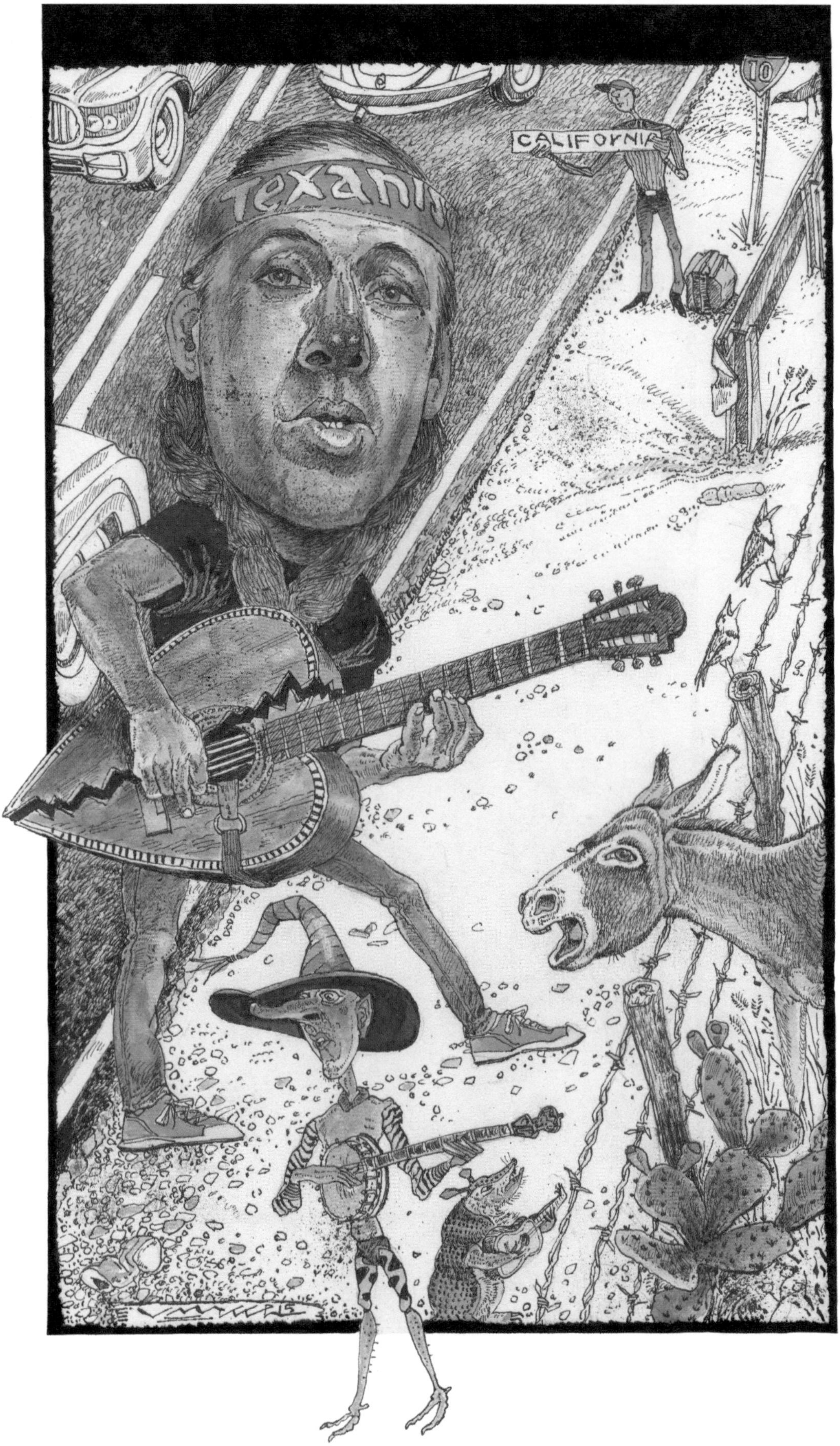
10
CALIFORNIA

Q: I just found out that the boy I've been dating for the past month and a half not only doesn't like Willie Nelson's music but actually dislikes his politics and everything else about him. Other than this, I have found him to be a pretty flawless guy. But is not liking Willie a deal killer? NAME WITHHELD, LUBBOCK

A: In all the years the Texanist has been doling out advice to those in need of it, he doesn't recall having ever been confronted with a situation quite like the strange and troubling one you have presented to him here. But then he's never in his whole life come across anyone quite like this beau with whom you've been carrying on recently. The Texanist isn't sure where you'd even meet a person like this. And he's spent time in some of the world's seedier cantinas, discotheques, and all-night truck-stop cafes. Even among the most unsavory acquaintances he's had the displeasure of making in these shabby dens, he's never met anyone who holds Willie Nelson in such low regard. Of course, everyone is entitled to their own musical proclivities. The Texanist, for example, is an admitted Wayne Newton fan. (Hey, it's his knocking-back-a-scotch-with-a-splash-of-water-and-two-ice-cubes-while-shining-up-for-a-night-on-the-town music! So what?) But disliking Willie—as a singer, a songwriter, an outlaw (of the mostly harmless variety), an unabashed Mary Jane enthusiast, and an incomparable treasure to all of humanity—speaks to your dude's character. What's this guy's deal, anyway? Nobody is here to tell anybody that somebody has to appreciate a particular musical artist as a prerequisite to being anybody's boyfriend, but by shunning Willie's transcendent tunesmithing, ever-pleasant warble, and overall munificence, this fellow has really shown himself to be, at the very least, a birdbrain. In short, you'd have to be crazy (see what the Texanist did there?) to continue in this doomed relationship. If you'd like, the Texanist would be happy to make the phone call for you.

Q: My husband and I graduated from what is now Texas State University on a Saturday and married the next day 19 years ago this past December. We then promptly moved to Florida for my hubby's career. Whenever we are asked where we are from, we always say that we are Texans living in Florida. But recently my husband responded that we were from Florida. The horror! Will you please explain to him why this cannot continue?
SUNI (AND CURTIS) PARKS, JACKSONVILLE, FLORIDA

A: The very first letter the Texanist ever responded to, way back in July 2007, was an inquiry that involved just this subject. The place from which one hails can be an integral part of one's general makeup and can say a lot about a person. It's important information to both get from someone and give to someone. And conveying it properly is crucial. From boardrooms to barrooms to bedrooms, the "Where are you from?" inquiry is a standard of introductory small talk, and whenever it is made, the questionee ought to be able to look his or her questioner in the eye and clearly, plainly, and hopefully proudly say the name of some place. As the Texanist pointed out to Texas-born New York resident Kate von der Porten in that inaugural bit of fine advice, there are contextual nuances to consider, but your own response— "We are Texans living in Florida"—is perfecto for your particular case. Your husband's recent misstep is troubling, though. The Texanist fears that his brainpan may have become sun damaged after those near two decades of life in the Sunshine State and that this may be the cause of his confusing the place where he currently resides (Florida) with the place from whence he came (Texas). These are two very different places. The Texanness you and your husband possess comes with no expiration date, but each individual holder is responsible for maintaining its upkeep. It would be a shame for him to unwittingly forfeit his by responding to the simplest of questions inaccurately. Perhaps it's time to saddle up and head on home for a spell. ★

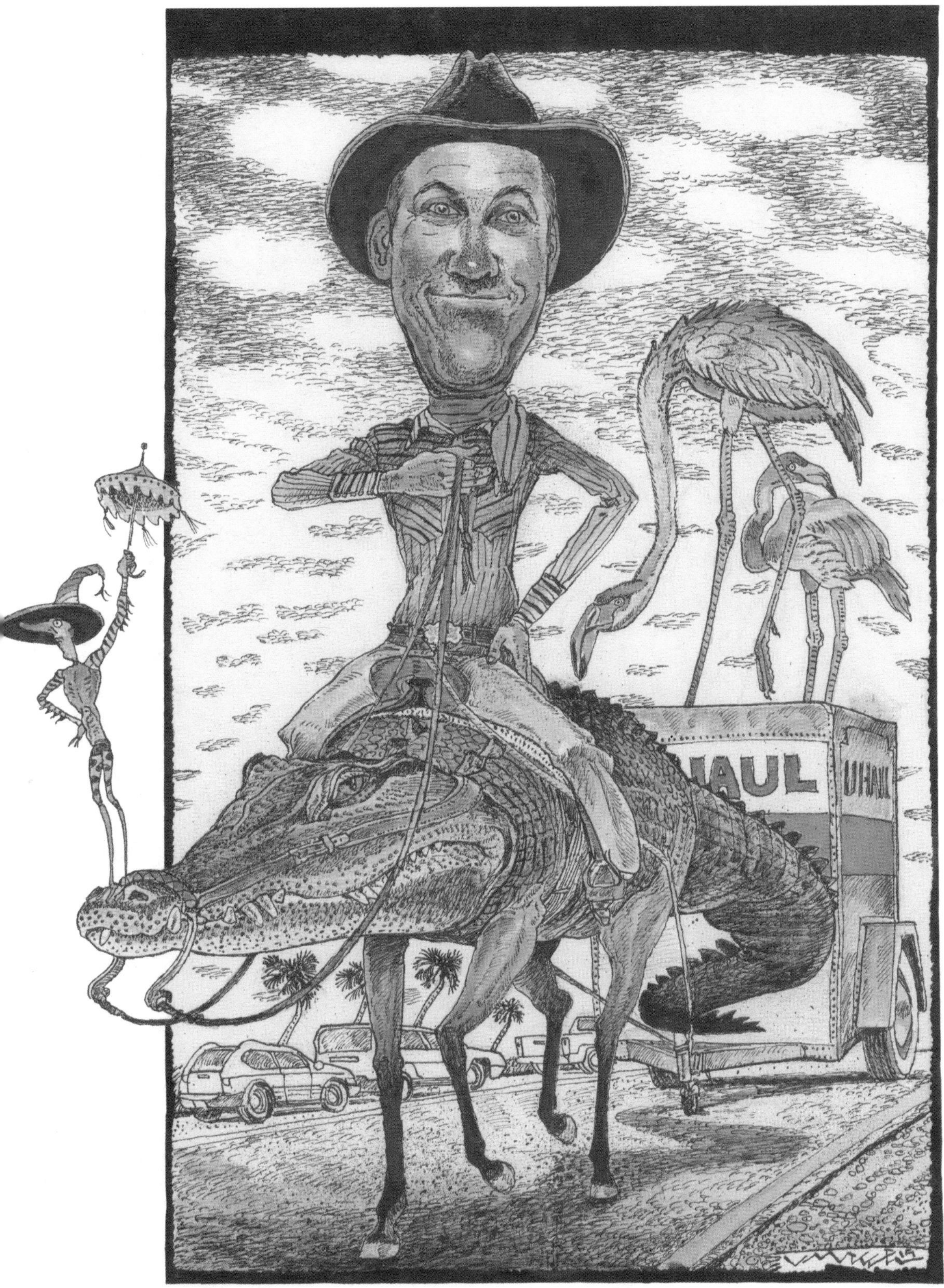
HAUL
UHAUL

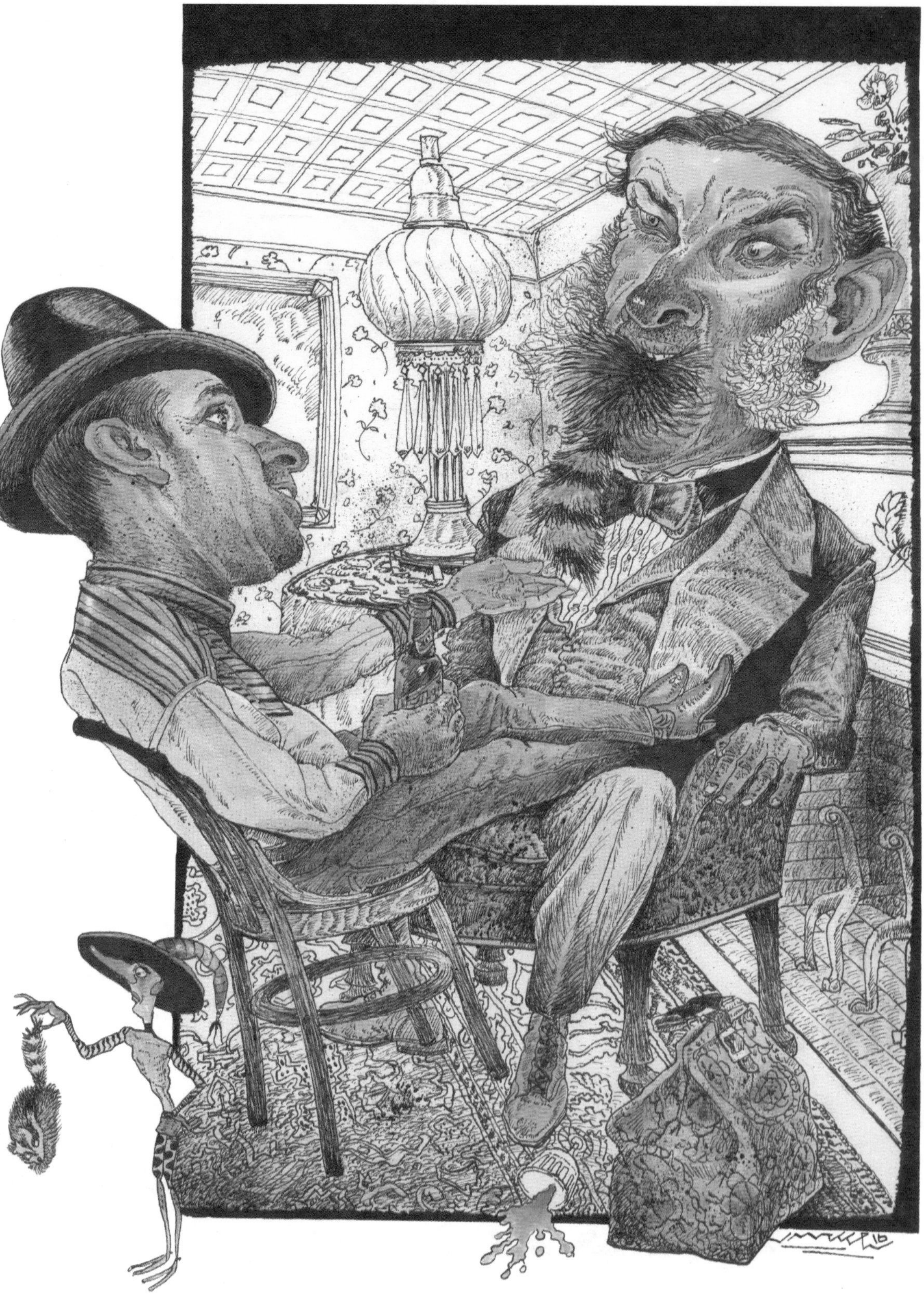

Q: My very close friend, who is a current Texas resident, constantly gives his home state of Tennessee credit for the "birth of Texas." Tennessee played a part, of course, but I'd like to rightsize his claim. Sam Houston wasn't even a native of the Volunteer State; he was Virginia-born. Our great state is the spawn of many nations (six flags), and that doesn't even include the Native American tribes that called this land home. What is it that keeps this Tennessean bragging and carrying on? MARTY B., AUSTIN

A: Your letter has reminded the Texanist of an invitation he once came across while perusing the *General Laws of the State of Texas Passed at the Regular Session of the Thirtieth Legislature, 1907.* In the spring of that year, via a joint resolution passed by its General Assembly, the state of Tennessee, in one of the largest doses of flowered-up braggadocio the Texanist has ever come across, summoned dispersed Tennesseans to Nashville for "Tennessee Home-coming Week": "Whereas the State of Tennessee stands preeminent as the mother State of the great Southwest, having furnished the States of Texas, Arkansas, and Missouri with their 'bone and sinew,' [*yada, yada*] glorious memory of Tennessee [*yada, yada*] those sons and daughters who peopled their lands with Crocketts and Houstons . . ." Sheesh! The Texanist, imagining your friend spouting forth similarly from a perch on your living room coffee table after having imbibed beyond his capacity, feels your pain. Yes, Tennessee and Texas are inextricably linked. This is an indisputable fact of history with which everybody is already familiar. Why your Tennessean friend feels the need to give his home state *full* credit for Texas's existence is as beyond the Texanist as it is you. Tennesseans, as we all know and as you acknowledge, played an important role. But, as you point out, so did many, many other non-Tennesseans. Your friend has gone too far. Does he also credit Tennessee for the birth of Willie Nelson because he happened to have worked in Nashville for a short period? Rather than advising you to quiet your friend with his own coonskin, the Texanist would like to invite the two of you down to the Menger Bar so that we can, preferably in the magniloquent parlance of that Tennessee homecoming invitation, hash this out further. ⋆

Q: I grew up in Ohio but have happily called myself a Texan for more than thirty years. I do not currently own any guns, but in light of the times in which we find ourselves, I've been thinking about arming myself and even getting a license to carry. My wife insists that this is a bad idea. I seek your counsel. NAME WITHHELD, VIA E-MAIL

A: Arming oneself with the goal of personal safety in mind is a decision that shouldn't be taken lightly, so the Texanist is glad that you have reached out. While he is not officially licensed to make determinations about a person's gun-worthiness, he's gotten pretty good at sizing up the folks who cross his path. Unfortunately, considering that he doesn't know your name or physical location, other than being somewhere in the 268,596 square miles of Texas vastness, he will be unable to make a ruling today. So as not to leave you hanging, though, the Texanist will tell you that, personally speaking, he is a man who favors the sunny side of the street and doesn't find the times so bad as to call for the mass toting of guns. This is not to say that guns shouldn't necessarily be toted. The Texanist has toted occasionally since he was a young man, but his shooting has always been done in the pursuit of recreation. Of course, it is your right to buy a gun, regardless of the reason. But just because a person can do something doesn't mean that person ought to do something. For example, the Texanist knows many old boys and girls who tote guns who, for a variety of reasons, he wishes didn't. The Texanist is sorry to have been unable to give your plan a stamp of approval, but he just doesn't have the information to do so at this time. Until further notice, he would encourage you to listen to your wife, a person who is better equipped than anybody to size you up properly. ★

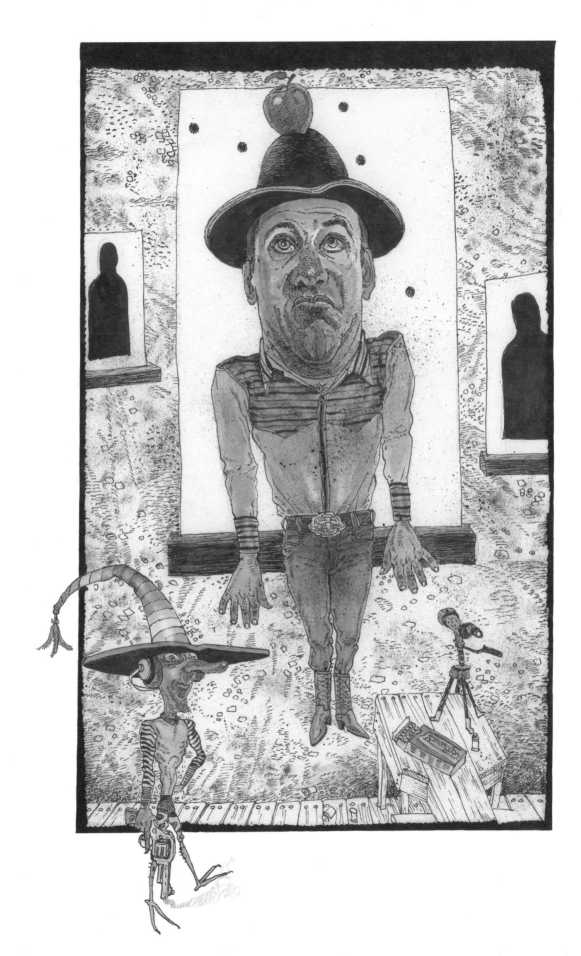

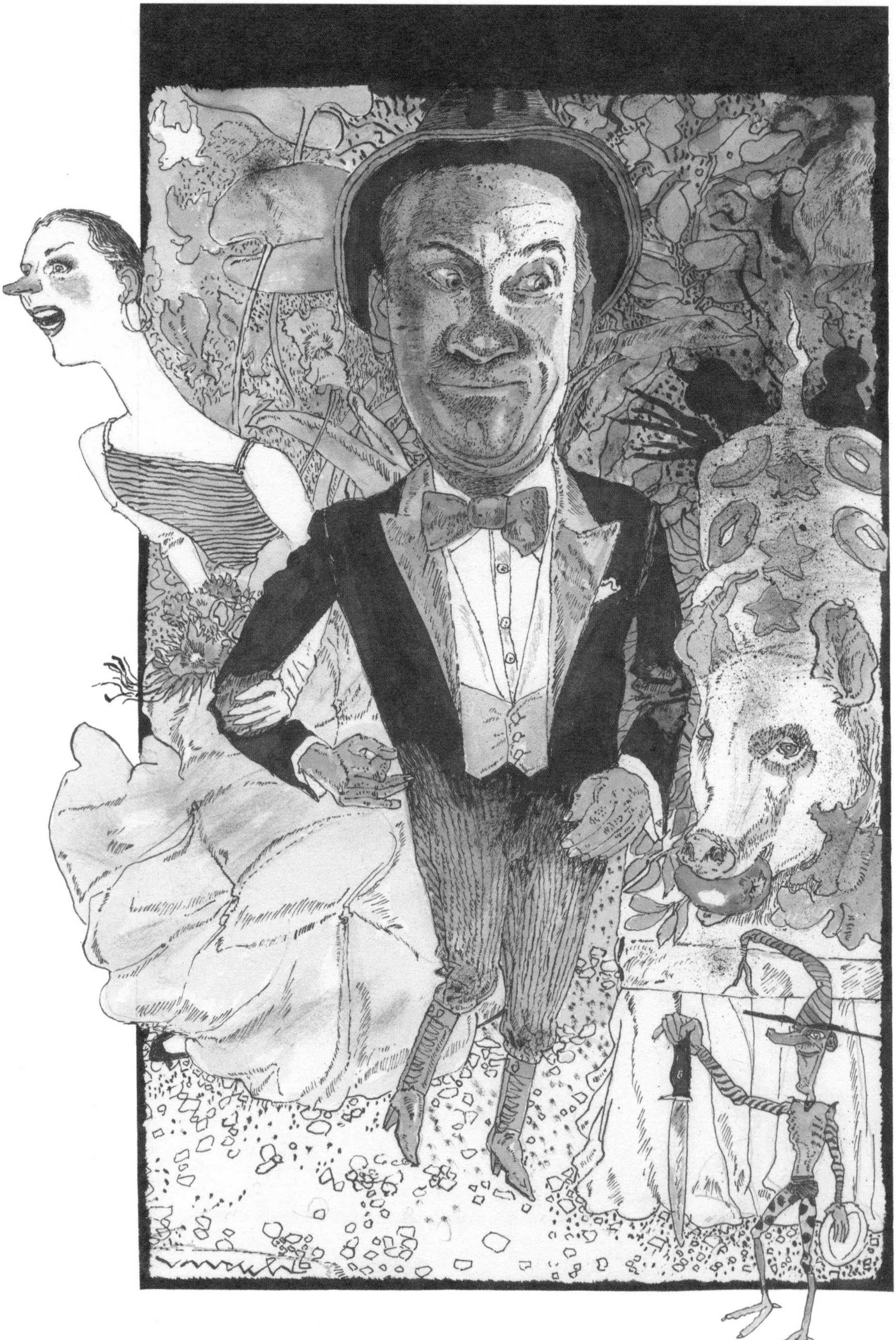

Q: The woman I am engaged to is an animal lover nonpareil, with three dogs, two cats, and a tankful of exotic fish in her care. As we live in a rural area, she also keeps an eye on a fox, numerous deer, countless birds, and an assortment of rodents. Against my advice, she has now asked her sister for a miniature Vietnamese potbellied pig as a wedding gift. Does this sound like a good idea? NAME WITHHELD, SAN ANTONIO

A: It's been a long time, but the Texanist seems to recall the most exotic item on his then bride-to-be's wedding registry wish list being an exorbitantly priced pepper mill from Williams-Sonoma. How the Texanist even survived all those years on canned pre-ground pepper is a mystery that confounds him to this day. But you've come with your own conundrum: the impending arrival of a miniature Vietnamese potbellied pig. Whether this idea is a good one or a bad one is a moot point. (Don't tell the future Mrs. Name Withheld, but it sounds like a very bad one to the Texanist.) Look, your fiancée's predilection for keeping pets of all makes and models is something you must have been well aware of during y'all's courtship. The smell alone had to have been a dead give-away. So seeing as you were undeterred then, putting your foot down now would be a tricky undertaking. In fact, with all the paws, hooves, claws, fins, and tails you'd have to be careful of in doing so, it would be damn near impossible. The Texanist apologizes for making light of your situation, but he couldn't help himself. And, unfortunately, he can't help you either. While you were probably hoping for some kind of novel advice involving a hot bed of coals and a rotisserie, there's simply nothing to be done at this point. But on the bright side, there's the chance that one day, years down the road, you'll wonder, as the Texanist sometimes does about the joys of fresh-ground pepper, what life was like before the love of that pet miniature Vietnamese potbellied pig. Congratulations to you and your bride. And welcome to the menagerie.

★

Facing: Last Illustration Unruh ever completed.